TOM'S DINER

TOM SMALLWOOD is a self-taught chef whose love for cooking began in childhood, helping his mum and grandma in the kitchen. Without formal training, he carved his own path in hospitality, learning through hands-on experience and embracing a 'learn as you go' mindset. Passionate about making food approachable, Tom shares simple, tasty recipes to inspire others – especially young people – to get cooking. With a combined following of over one million on Instagram, TikTok and YouTube (@tom.smallwood), he shows his community that delicious meals don't need to be complicated or fancy. Tom's goal is to make home cooking fun, creative and something anyone can feel confident doing, no matter their experience level.

PLEASE
'BREAK DOWN'
YOUR
BOXES

TOM'S DINER

TOM SMALLWOOD

PENGUIN BOOKS

UK | USA | Canada | Ireland | Australia
India | New Zealand | South Africa | China

Penguin Books is part of the Penguin Random House group of companies
whose addresses can be found at global.penguinrandomhouse.com

Penguin
Random House
Australia

First published by Penguin Books in 2025

Cover and internal photography by William Meppem
Cover and internal design by Kirby Armstrong © Penguin Random House Australia Pty Ltd
Illustrations by alyonaz/Shutterstock (lasagna), AVA Bitter/Shutterstock (pot), DrawUrLife/
Shutterstock (pizza), Foxy Fox/Shutterstock (patterns and mascots), Johnny14/Shutterstock
(lasagna), roughedges_stock/Shutterstock (muffin), seamartini/iStock (kitchenware), shockfactor/
Shutterstock (steak), tanyabosyk/Shutterstock (mascots), user0511982/Shutterstock (ketchup),
Victoria Sergeeva/Shutterstock (bottles)
Food styling by Lucy Tweed
Typeset in Calluna and Greycliff CF by Post Pre-press Group, Australia

Printed and bound in China by 1010 Printing International Co. Ltd

A catalogue record for this
book is available from the
National Library of Australia

ISBN 978 1 76135 373 4

We at Penguin Random House Australia acknowledge that Aboriginal and Torres Strait Islander
peoples are the Traditional Custodians and the first storytellers of the lands on which we live
and work. We honour Aboriginal and Torres Strait Islander peoples' continuous connection
to Country, waters, skies and communities. We celebrate Aboriginal and Torres Strait Islander
stories, traditions and living cultures, and we pay our respects to Elders past and present.

This one's for you, Pascal . . .
there are a lot of idiots in this world
and this one wrote a cookbook.

CONTENTS

CHAPTER 1
Handheld Faves

CHAPTER 2
(Almost) One Pan Wonders

HOW IT ALL BEGAN

I always knew I wanted to be a chef . . .

. . . is how I would love to start this book, but in reality, I kind of stumbled into a kitchen one day and just never left. Food has always been a HUGE part of any event in my family. My grandma, aunty and mum would cook these grand meals for Christmas and go all out with the roast meats and potatoes. We would all sit around the same table and talk for hours – well, really it was the adults talking over the top of each other and us kids waiting to be excused from the table. Grandma always made sure there was so much food, too much food to be honest, but those times spent around the table really cemented the importance of food and how it brought us all together.

I really didn't want to be working in a kitchen – in fact, I didn't know what I wanted. My first experience in a commercial kitchen was when my older sister got me a job washing dishes at the local golf club bistro in 2014. The head chef there, Pascal, was a real hard-ass and the stereotypical 'French chef', yelling the house down when things were falling apart and even throwing things across the kitchen! To be honest I don't actually think he ever threw anything, but I like to remember it that way. Pascal scared the shit out of me for the first two years I worked for him because I was just a kid and he was this angry French man who, despite having lived in Australia for 25 years, still spoke in slightly broken English. I can't count the amount of times he would be talking to me and half-way through the sentence switch to French and then expect me to have a clue about what he was saying.

Once I finished school without a clue where I was going in life, I enrolled in an online uni course and didn't do a single assessment. Great way to waste $7,000 that you don't have as an 18-year-old. My mum suggested (made me) apply for a kitchen-hand position in a pastry kitchen. We were family friends with the owners, and I got the job and subsequently left my prestigious roll as CDW (chief of dish washing) at the golf club. I learnt a lot about the world of a pastry chef and quickly realized that it's absolutely rubbish. These guys (and girls) worked so insanely hard, some of them coming into work at 2 am. I knew this wasn't for me, I really didn't like it at all. The owners were always very nice to me but I was scared of them in a different way to Pascal. One morning I walked into the news that I had, accidentally, left 15 large pies out of the fridge overnight and they were ruined. These pies sold for roughly $30 each and I wished the floor would open up and swallow me so I didn't have to deal with the repercussions. The owners, Vicky and Tracey, didn't scream at me, but if I was them I would have wanted to (sorry again, guys!). It was around this time that my dreams of being a YouTube sensation came to life, though it wasn't until I left this job that I started making content.

When I said I kind of stumbled into a kitchen, I really meant that I never sought out kitchen work, it just kind of found me. My third job in a kitchen was offered to me by a friend whose mum owned a cafe in Sutton Forrest called Eling Forest Winery Cafe. It was a cute, rustic cafe just off the highway that got insanely busy because it was the only place to get real food between Sydney and Goulburn without having to make a detour, apart from McDonald's. I had started making random YouTube videos and the owner, Janelle, found out. Instead of making fun of me like a lot of others would, she supported me. She would play my videos on a loop on the cafe computer all day and she even gave me my first studio light box to make my videos better.

I don't think I ever really got to thank Janelle enough for the support she gave me; she was my first real fan. I was working in the cafe kitchen for a few months before the head chef left and the entire kitchen operation was left to myself and another 18-year-old, Harry, who is still one of my good mates. This time was literally mayhem: we were two kids who could barely keep up with the prep list, let alone the ordering and trying to think of something new to add to the specials board each week. I think we had a vegetable frittata on the specials board for a month straight. Pair all of that with an oven that turned itself off every 20 minutes and a leaky roof that would drip into the deep fryer and that's a recipe for success if you ask me. In order to split up the limited kitchen staff (the two of us!) we had to have a day alone in the kitchen each per week and I didn't cope but I feel like I did my best. It was the biggest 'sink or swim' experience that I've had in my life and aside from the tremendous anxiety I would feel on the morning of my solo 'chef' day, once I got into the breakfast rush, I entered into a flow state (if you think of a flow state as constantly telling Janelle that I'm stressed and can't handle this).

This period of my life felt so stressful at the time but looking back, I wouldn't change a thing. Eventually we got more kitchen staff, some real qualified chefs and I got the call up from the big man himself, Pascal, to come and work for him again in the cafe he had just bought with his son and daughter, Nic and Chloe.

I was still chasing my dreams of becoming a YouTuber by any means possible. If anyone reading this remembers the 'Aussie comedy Tom', I really appreciate you so much but please, let's bury those memories!

Working for Pascal in his French cafe, The Kookabar, completely changed my relationship with cooking. I went from a stressful environment in a hot and busy kitchen to a stressful environment in a hot and busy kitchen but with classic rock playing on the radio and a big, bald Frenchman smoking cigarettes in one breath out the back. To me that's objectively better. Jokes aside, the next five years working under him changed my life. My YouTube dreams were dwindling and I had everyone around me asking, 'Why don't you start making cooking videos?'. My answer was that I didn't want to be spending all day cooking to then come home and set up the camera to cook more. You wouldn't expect a carpet layer to come home after a long day and start laying more carpet, right? But the real answer was that I didn't want Pascal to see my level of cooking and judge me. I might not have ever started posting food content online if he didn't tell me that he originally wanted to be a firefighter but ended up being a chef instead and a pretty damn good one, too. This made me realize that your first choice isn't always the best choice.

I decided to really lean into the cooking because I felt like I could make an impact on younger people who didn't know how to cook, just like myself only a few years earlier. I would spend all day asking him questions about the food he was making: 'Why do you add that in now?', 'How do you know when this is done?' or 'Why are you bald?'. I asked him so many questions that he would often reply, 'Why you ask so many f***ing questions?' or just flat out ignore me. Over time and thousands of questions I began to learn so much – techniques, flavour combinations, intuition and, most importantly, how to say curse words in French.

I made the change from posting whatever trending content there was online to straight up home cooking content and my first video did well enough that I never looked back. It wasn't long before I was

running lunch service at the cafe – some might call it 'head chef' but I don't have any qualification, so I privately called myself *El Jefe*. There was definitely a sense of self-importance about that, but I would always try to keep my cool because Pascal would flip his lid for me. This was where I really grew my understanding for the food we were preparing, and it all started to make sense and feel 'simple'.

I began to develop and understand my own process and this directly translated into my content, which started performing much better. Pascal, like Janelle, supported my content and even though he wanted it to seem like he didn't care, I know he did. I would be sent home with French recipes like chocolate mousse (which is in this book) and countless serving dishes to present my French works of art. I didn't care as much what the comments were saying, I only cared about his critique, making him watch the video I posted the night before or eat the leftovers I brought in to win his approval. I would be over the moon if he said 'This is good, mate' – he had such a way with words!

Eventually, I was at a point where my content was performing well enough to support myself financially, so I began to reduce the amount of hours I was working at the cafe and I almost regret it a little. However stressful and hot the kitchen got, if everyone spent the whole day angry at each other and just wanting it to end, we all understood that at the end of the day it was over and we were friends again. That's what I miss the most about working in a kitchen.

Pascal taught me almost everything I know about cooking, and he sparked my love for the process of it. Without him taking me under his sweaty French wing I have no idea where I would be, but I know that I wouldn't ever have been able to write this cookbook. He's probably going to read this and call me an idiot but I don't care, this is my cookbook and I'll say what I want.

Thanks for everything, Pascal, love you, mate!

Now that you're caught up to speed with my kitchen life, let's talk about why this book exists.

Apart from the natural sense of progression as an online 'foodie' to write a recipe book, I wanted to create something that conveys how I think when I'm cooking. The natural step-by-step process that I go through to simplify a recipe. If you flick through the chapters you will see that the recipes follow similar steps even if the outcome is different. Maybe I had to simplify everything down because I'm a bit slow and can't handle too much at once, but I hope that you can use this as a tool to advance your cooking capabilities and become more confident in your kitchen, no matter who you're cooking for. More importantly, I want you to ENJOY COOKING.

I've split the book into five chapters ranging from quick 15-minute snacks to delicious meals that are sure to impress that special someone. This book is for anyone and everyone who likes to cook or wants to learn how to cook better. I still have so much to learn, but what I do know is how to elevate everyday dishes from a boring weeknight meal to something that will make your friends want the recipe.

Chapter 1: Handheld Faves

I'm a lazy guy, so I'll try to find the easiest way to do something. This chapter is full of my favourite foods that you can pick up and rip into. Think pizzas, tacos, burgers and sandwiches.

Chapter 2: (Almost) One Pan Wonders

If you're short on time or just don't want to be in the kitchen for ages, then this is the chapter for you. These recipes are the epitome of how my brain works when cooking. Using simple cooking techniques to add flavour and give you a delicious meal, all in one pan (plus maybe a pot for boiling water).

Chapter 3: Elevated Basics

'Girls love a guy who can cook' is often thrown around, but what if you can't cook?! Follow these recipes and your date night will be a great night. If you've got some extra time on your hands or just enjoy making more elaborate meals, I've selected some of my favourite, more time-consuming meals that will have your guests wanting more.

Chapter 4: A Little Sweet Treat

If no one in the world wants a little sweet treat, I'm dead. I really love desserts, maybe from my time in the pastry kitchen or learning how to make the perfect crème anglaise. There's just an itch that only something sweet will scratch. These are some of my all-time favourite desserts and I know you'll absolutely love them.

Chapter 5: Flavour Foundations

In this chapter, I will give you tips on how to set up your kitchen, staples that you can make ahead of time to keep in the pantry or fridge, what's in my spice rack, tips on how I do the groceries and helpful kitchen cheat sheets.

All oven temperatures listed are in conventional ovens. If you are using a fan-forced oven, reduce the listed temperature by 20°C.

MY ESSENTIAL KITCHEN EQUIPMENT

I don't think you need a million pots and pans to be able to cook well. I do however think that using the correct equipment can change a meal. I predominantly use stainless steel or cast-iron cookware because of the heat retention and durability and I would love to jump onto the band wagon that Teflon has no place in any kitchen, but I still own and use one single non-stick pan. Here is my list of the essential equipment and utensils that I think should be in every home kitchen, and an extended list of extra things that just make things a bit easier.

COOKING EQUIPMENT

Barebones

FRYING PANS OF DIFFERENT SIZES

This includes a 30-cm stainless steel frying pan, a 20–22-cm cast-iron frying pan and a 24-cm nonstick frying pan.

LARGE STAINLESS-STEEL POT (AT LEAST 5 L)

Perfect for making stock, cooking pasta or soups and Bolognese-style mixtures.

STAINLESS STEEL MIXING BOWLS

20 cm, 25 cm and 28 cm.

WOODEN CHOPPING BOARD

My chopping board is 50 × 34 × 5 cm. I would suggest a thicker board for durability, this size board has more than enough surface area for any prep work you'll be doing.

BAKING TRAYS

Depending on the size of your oven you'll need different-sized baking trays, but regardless, they NEED to be thick! Thinner trays can warp in the heat of the oven and could misshape whatever it is that you're cooking.

WIRE RACKS

These go hand-in-hand with baking trays. As well as for cooling baked goods, wire racks that fit inside your baking trays are perfect for draining oil from fried foods or allowing airflow for evenly roasted meats.

LARGE SIEVE

My choice is a large fine mesh sieve. You can use it to strain stock, sift flour and drain pasta.

Extras

DUTCH OVEN, WHICH IS ENAMELLED CAST IRON

Le Creuset is a good brand and will last a lifetime but is very expensive. There are alternative brands which will still do a very good job.

2.4 L STAINLESS STEEL SAUCEPAN WITH LID

This stainless steel saucepan will be an absolute workhorse in your kitchen and can be used for anything from frying an egg to cooking a pasta bake in the oven. A pan like this is one of the most important pieces of equipment you'll have.

23 CM GLASS MIXING BOWL

Make sure it's heat treated (borosilicate glass). If buying PYREX make sure it's the one with the all-caps logo. The others are made of different glass.

BLENDER

I think a high-powered blender that has both a standard blender jug and smaller blender cups is best, mainly for the versatility. Most things can be achieved with this blender set up.

FOOD PROCESSOR

Great for making pastry quickly, as well as chopping things that you want to keep some texture in.

BAKING DISH/ROASTING PAN

30 × 20 cm porcelain for baking, cast iron for roasting meats and vegetables.

IMMERSION BLENDER

This is one of those things that once you have it, you'll wonder how you ever lived without it. From making mayonnaise to blending soups in the pot, it's easier than getting out the big blender, and makes for easier clean up.

COOKING UTENSILS

Barebones

18–20 CM CHEF'S KNIFE

This is a perfect all-rounder and is great for most things.

9 CM PARING KNIFE

The Victorinox ones are great in my opinion, they cost around $10 and feel indestructible. You can use these for anything.

SCISSORS

A strong set of kitchen scissors is ESSENTIAL. Sometimes when I'm too lazy to wash a cutting board I'll chop my chicken with scissors.

MEASURING SPOONS

A standard set has ¼ teaspoon, ½ teaspoon, 1 teaspoon and 1 tablespoon.

A WOODEN SPOON

I like to use a wooden spoon when I'm cooking longer-cooked dishes because they don't heat up like metal utensils. You can leave it in a hot pot and not have to worry about burning your hand when you pick it up again.

MICROPLANE

This is definitely one of my most used pieces of equipment, you can grate garlic without making your chopping board smell for days, garnish your pastas with freshly grated parmesan and finely grate citrus zest.

TONGS

I think you should have two pairs. One around 24 cm long and another around 30 cm long, The longer ones are especially good for the barbecue, keeping your hand further from the heat.

BENCH SCRAPER

Whether it's a stainless steel bench scraper or just a simple plastic one, these things are indispensable. From gathering up chopped foods to transfer into a pan to cleaning the bench, it's just one of those little changes that can save time and ultimately make the cooking experience better.

SILICON SPATULA

Since working in commercial kitchens these are my favourite tool to use, specifically the Vogue high-heat resistant 'spoonula'. These spatulas can withstand heat up to 260°C and are almost indestructible. Get one, trust me.

SLOTTED SPOON OR WOK SKIMMER

A slotted spoon is okay, but a wok skimmer is really the best. Used for scooping food from liquid, it is the best utensil for deep-frying because it has enough surface area to scoop up anything, from popcorn chicken to donuts, while letting the oil drain back into the pan.

Extras

A HEAVY WHISK, WITH THICK WIRES AND A STRONG HANDLE

Spend a little more money and they won't break so easily.

ROLLING PIN

I prefer the traditional baker's rolling pin which is just a straight cylinder of wood. It's simple and does the job.

STAINLESS STEEL SPOON

I still don't own a ladle, but if I've made it this far without one I guess it's not really an essential. The thin material allows you to be more precise when skimming the fat off the top of a sauce, scooping ingredients and stirring. I would avoid using this on Teflon or enamel pots/pans.

STEEL SPATULA

There are some utensils that have specific jobs and they just do them really well. My stainless steel spatula is used for scooping things off baking trays, like roasted vegetables or cookies, but sometimes I just need something hard and straight-edged to scrape the mistakes off my stainless or cast-iron pans.

INTERNAL MEAT THERMOMETER

If you're someone who always overcooks steak or is cutting the chicken open in the pan to check if it's cooked, you need a meat thermometer, and digital is best. It really takes the guess work out of cooking meat. To check, insert it into the thickest part of the meat (avoiding any bone). If it doesn't reach the desired temperature, cook a bit longer then check again.

DEEP-FRYING THERMOMETER

Stand this in your pan of oil to keep an eye on the temperature so you can adjust the heat accordingly. Heat that is too low will make soggy, greasy food. Too high means the food will burn before it is cooked through. These usually double as a candy thermometer, so you can use them for caramel or toffee, and other liquid dishes such as custard.

KITCHEN SCALES

These aren't exclusively for the gym-bros, this is another indispensable piece of cooking equipment. I really don't like the inaccuracy of measuring in volume, that's why most of the recipes I post online have measurements in grams. It's just more accurate and a good set of kitchen scales will really help you nail any recipe.

Handheld Faves

Everything Dough

This is a dough that I use for everything from pizza bases to burger buns.
It's so versatile and with a few tweaks can be used for almost anything.

MAKES 5 pizzas or
10–12 bread rolls/burger buns
PREP TIME 10–15 minutes plus
1½ hours rising

400 g plain flour
200 g bread flour
7 g sachet dry yeast
6 g sugar
6 g salt
375 g tepid water (30–35°C)
55 g olive oil

1 Combine both flours, yeast, sugar and salt in a large bowl and whisk to combine. Create a small well in the centre.

2 Pour in the water and olive oil. Using a knife or flat spatula, make cutting motions to incorporate all the ingredients. When a shaggy ball of dough forms, turn it out onto the bench and knead for 5-10 minutes, until you have a smooth ball of dough. Lightly oil a clean bowl and place the dough in it. Cover and leave for 1 hour or until doubled in size

3 From here the world is your oyster. If you want to turn it into:

PIZZA BASES Divide into 5 equal portions (roughly 200 g each), roll tightly into balls and leave, covered, to rise for another 30 minutes before stretching into pizza bases. For a deeper flavour, I suggest you place each portion in its own container and leave in the fridge to cold ferment for 2–4 days. Proceed with your favourite pizza recipe.

BREAD ROLLS/BURGER BUNS Divide into 10–12 equal portions and roll tightly into balls. Arrange onto baking trays. Stand, covered, for 30 minutes to rise. Meanwhile preheat the oven to 180°C. Brush with lightly beaten egg and bake for 20–25 minutes, until golden brown. Cool on a wire rack.

Pizza-stuffed Pull-apart Garlic Bread

Whenever I get invited to a dinner event and they say 'just bring something', my first and only thought is to make some form of garlic bread. This recipe is tried and tested on all of my friends (multiple times). They love it so I know you will too.

MAKES 18
PREP TIME 30 minutes plus
   30 minutes rising
COOK TIME 20–25 minutes
   plus cooling

1 quantity Everything Dough (page 3)
300 g low-moisture mozzarella,
   cut into 18 cubes
150 g pepperoni, diced
1 egg
garlic and herb butter (optional,
   page 197)

Low-moisture mozzarella is firmer than fresh mozzarella, such as buffalo mozzarella (which you would get in a tub of brine). You just want the standard supermarket mozz, perfect for this recipe as it is not so wet.

1 Punch down the dough after rising. Turn out onto a work surface and divide into 18 equal portions. Roll each portion into a small ball, then flatten each ball with your hands or a rolling pin into a round disc. Place a cube of mozzarella and a few pieces of diced pepperoni in the centre of each disc. Carefully fold the edges of the dough around the filling. Pinch the seams together tightly to ensure the filling is sealed completely, so it won't leak out during baking.

2 Grease two 23 cm square cake pans or baking dishes with oil, or line with baking paper. Arrange the stuffed dough balls in the prepared pans, join-side down, placing them snugly next to each other. Cover the pans with a clean tea towel or plastic wrap and let them rise in a warm place for 30 minutes, or until they have puffed up and nearly doubled in size.

3 Meanwhile, preheat the oven to 180°C. Prepare an egg wash by whisking the egg with a tablespoon of water.

4 Once the rolls have risen, lightly brush the tops with the egg wash for a golden finish. Bake for 20–25 minutes or until golden brown on top. If your oven has hot spots, rotate the pans halfway through baking for even colouring. Remove the rolls from the oven and, while they are still hot, brush the tops with garlic and herb butter for added flavour (optional).

5 Allow the stuffed bread rolls to cool for 10–15 minutes before serving. This will help the cheese set inside and prevent burns when biting into them. Serve as pictured or straight from the pans.

6 Leftover rolls can be stored in an airtight container at room temperature for up to 2 days. These rolls freeze well too! Allow them to cool completely before wrapping tightly in plastic wrap and storing in a freezer-safe bag for up to 3 months. To reheat, bake from frozen at 180°C for 10–15 minutes.

Cheese-
burger
Spring
Rolls

Cheeseburger Spring Rolls

What do you get when you take the flavours from a cheeseburger, wrap
them up tightly and deep-fry them in a crispy shell? An unbeatable appetiser.
I've given you the choice to either air-fry or deep-fry these – whatever works for you!

MAKES 20
PREP TIME 30 minutes
COOK TIME 15–20 minutes

20 spring roll wrappers
300 g low-moisture mozzarella,
  cut into 20 sticks roughly
  1 cm x 1 cm x 10 cm
¼ red onion, diced
vegetable oil (if deep-frying)
cooking oil spray (if air-frying)

BEEF FILLING
500 g beef mince
1 tablespoon sweet paprika
1 teaspoon onion powder
1 teaspoon garlic powder
1 teaspoon beef stock powder
1 teaspoon sea salt
1 teaspoon freshly ground black
  pepper

DIPPING SAUCE
⅔ cup (200 g) mayonnaise
¼ cup (35g) diced pickles
1 tablespoon pickle juice or
  white vinegar
½ teaspoon dijon mustard
1 teaspoon sweet paprika
¼ teaspoon onion powder
¼ teaspoon garlic powder

1 To make the beef filling, heat a large frying pan over medium-high heat.
   Add the beef mince and cook, breaking up with a spatula, until browned
   and fully cooked through. Season the beef with paprika, onion powder,
   garlic powder, beef stock powder, salt and pepper. Stir to combine and
   allow to cool slightly before using.

2 For the dipping sauce, in a small bowl, combine mayonnaise, pickles,
   pickle juice or vinegar, mustard, paprika, onion powder and garlic
   powder. Mix thoroughly and set aside.

3 To assemble, lay one spring roll wrapper flat on a clean work surface
   with one corner facing you (diamond shape). In the centre of the
   wrapper, spoon roughly 2 tbsp of the cooked beef mince, a stick of
   mozzarella, and a sprinkle of diced red onion. Add a teaspoon of the
   prepared dipping sauce on top of the filling. Fold in the sides of the
   wrapper and then carefully roll it up from the bottom. Once rolled,
   lightly brush the top edge with a bit of water to seal the spring roll.
   Repeat with remaining ingredients.

4 To air-fry: Preheat the air-fryer to 180°C. Lightly spray each spring roll
   with cooking oil and arrange in a single layer in the air-fryer basket,
   ensuring they are not touching. Cook for 8–10 minutes or until golden
   brown and crispy, turning halfway through for even cooking.

   To deep-fry: Half-fill an large pot or deep-fryer with oil and heat to
   180°C. Fry the spring rolls in batches for about 4–5 minutes, or until
   they are golden and crispy. Be sure to turn them occasionally for even
   cooking. Use a slotted spoon to transfer to a paper towel-lined plate to
   drain any excess oil. Immediately sprinkle lightly with salt while still hot.

5 Serve the spring rolls warm, with the dipping sauce on the side.

Using too much water to seal spring roll
wrappers can cause uneven browning
or burning during frying. Keep the
water minimal, just enough to seal the
edges for even, crispy results.

Chips and Dips

I love going to restaurants that bring out hot bread or chips and dips when you didn't even ask for them. I know that you end up paying for it but it's the little things that make the whole experience better. These three dips feel like the holy trinity of scoopable sauces – creamy guac, cheesy queso and spicy salsa all scooped up on some homemade corn chips!! If you put these on my table, I'm going to town on them.

OVEN-BAKED CORN CHIPS

SERVES 3–4
PREP TIME 10 minutes
COOK TIME 12 minutes

6–8 corn tortillas
2 tablespoons olive oil
½ teaspoon salt

1   Preheat the oven to 180°C.

2   Stack the corn tortillas and cut them into
6–8 wedges (like a pizza). Arrange the wedges in
a single layer on a large baking tray. You may need
two baking trays depending on the size.

3   Drizzle the oil over the tortilla wedges. Sprinkle with
salt and toss to evenly coat.

4   Bake for 10–12 minutes, or until the chips are golden
brown and crispy. Be sure to keep an eye on them in
the last few minutes to prevent burning.

5   Cool slightly before serving. This will allow them to
crisp up even more.

CREAMY GUACAMOLE

SERVES 3–4
PREP TIME 10 minutes

2 large, ripe avocados
1 clove garlic, finely grated
½ teaspoon salt (or to taste)
juice of ½ lime
2 tablespoons Greek yoghurt
thinly sliced coriander leaves, to serve

1   Cut the avocados in half. Remove the pit and scoop
the flesh into a medium bowl.

2   Using a fork, mash the avocado flesh until smooth,
leaving a bit of chunkiness if preferred for texture.

3   Add the garlic, salt, juice and yoghurt. Use a whisk
to vigorously stir the mixture for 1–2 minutes. This will
help aerate the guacamole, making it extra creamy
and light.

4   Sprinkle with the coriander leaves for an added
burst of freshness.

SALSA ROJA

SERVES 3–4
PREP TIME 15 minutes plus steeping
COOK TIME 5–7 minutes

3 Roma tomatoes
1 brown onion, peeled and roughly chopped
3 cloves garlic, peeled
2 dried guajillo chillies
1 dried bay leaf
2 teaspoons dried oregano
1 teaspoon salt
½ teaspoon ground black pepper
1–2 tablespoons olive oil (optional)

1　Use a small sharp knife to score the bottoms of the tomatoes with an 'X'. Place the scored tomatoes, onion and garlic into a saucepan and cover with cold water. Bring to the boil, reduce the heat slightly and simmer for 5–7 minutes, until the skins of the tomatoes begin to peel back. Remove the tomatoes, onion and garlic from the pan. When cool enough to handle, peel the skins off the tomatoes.

2　Meanwhile, in a small saucepan, bring a little water to a simmer. Add the chillies to the simmering water, turn the heat off, cover with a lid and let them steep for 10–15 minutes, or until soft and aromatic. Drain and remove the stems and seeds.

3　In a blender or food processor, combine the peeled tomatoes, onion, garlic, chillies, bay leaf, oregano, salt and pepper. Blend until you achieve your desired smoothness. If you like a smoother texture, blend longer.

4　For a richer, thicker sauce, you can slowly pour in the olive oil while the blender or food processor is running. This will slightly emulsify the sauce and change its colour from a deep red to a vibrant orange.

5　Taste the sauce and adjust the seasoning with additional salt and pepper as needed.

CHEESY QUESO DIP

SERVES 3–4
PREP TIME 10 minutes
COOK TIME 10 minutes

½ small brown onion, roughly chopped
2 cloves garlic, peeled
1 small jalapeño, deseeded and finely diced (optional)
1 tablespoon butter
2 teaspoons cornflour
⅔ cup (160 ml) evaporated milk
250 g cheddar cheese, grated
1 tablespoon smoked paprika
1 tablespoon ground cumin
½ cup coriander leaves, finely sliced

1　In a blender or food processor, combine the onion, garlic and jalapeño (if using). Blend until the mixture is slightly chunky.

2　In a small saucepan, melt the butter over medium heat. Add the onion mixture and sweat for 3–4 minutes, stirring frequently, until fragrant and softened.

3　In a small bowl, combine the cornflour and evaporated milk and stir until smooth. Pour into the saucepan with the onion mixture, stirring to combine. Bring the mixture to a gentle simmer and cook, stirring occasionally, for 2–3 minutes, until the sauce begins to thicken.

4　Add the grated cheese in batches, stirring slowly to melt the cheese completely after each addition. Continue until all the cheese has melted and the sauce is smooth.

5　Remove the saucepan from the heat. Stir in the smoked paprika, ground cumin and coriander leaves. Season with salt and freshly ground black pepper to taste.

6　If the queso is too thick, add a little more evaporated milk to reach your desired consistency. If the queso is too thin, dissolve another 2 teaspoons cornflour in a small amount of cold water, then slowly add it to the queso, a little at a time, until the sauce thickens to your liking. Serve warm.

Oven-Baked Corn Chips
Creamy Guacamole
Salsa Roja

Cheesy
Queso Dip

Mozzarella-stuffed Garlic Knots

These little pillowy pockets of baked bread are stuffed with mozzarella cheese and tossed through garlic butter. These taste how the stuffed crust pizza ads look!

MAKES about 30
PREP TIME 30 minutes
COOK TIME 20 minutes

200 g mozzarella, cut into 1 cm cubes
80 g butter, melted
40 g garlic butter, melted
2 tablespoons finely grated
   parmesan

DOUGH
7 g sachet dry yeast
6 g sugar
375 g tepid water (30–35°C)
400 g plain flour
200 g bread flour
55 g olive oil
6 g salt

Leftover knots can be stored in an airtight container in the fridge for up to two days. To reheat, place the knots in an oven at 180°C until warmed through. For long-term storage, freeze the knots in a single layer on a baking tray until firm, then transfer them to a freezer-safe bag or container. They can be kept in the freezer for up to 1 month. Reheat from frozen in the oven at 160°C for 10–12 minutes.

1   Preheat the oven to 200°C. Line a large baking tray with baking paper.

2   To make the dough, in the bowl of a stand mixer (or a large mixing bowl) combine the yeast, sugar and water. Stir the ingredients until they are well combined, then cover the bowl and let it sit for 10 minutes to allow the yeast to activate. The mixture should start to bubble and become frothy.

3   After 10 minutes, uncover the bowl and add the flour, olive oil and salt to the activated yeast mixture. Using a dough hook attachment (or by hand), mix the ingredients on low speed until they come together into a dough. Work the dough for 10 minutes until it becomes smooth and elastic. If kneading by hand, lightly flour the surface and knead until the dough is smooth and slightly tacky. Turn the dough out onto a lightly floured surface. Gently press into a flat rectangle about 1–1.5 cm thick.

4   Cut the dough vertically into 1.5 cm wide strips, then cut those strips in half horizontally to portion the dough into small pieces.

5   Take one strip of dough and gently stretch it to wrap around your finger, leaving no opening at the top. Place a cube of mozzarella at the tip of your finger, then invert the dough over the cheese, closing up the opening at the top of the knot. Place each stuffed dough knot onto a lined baking tray, making sure they are snug but not overcrowded.

6   Brush the knots lightly with melted butter and bake in the oven for 10–20 minutes, or until golden brown and slightly risen. The baking time may vary depending on your oven, so check the knots around the 10-minute mark. Rotate the tray halfway through if necessary for even browning.

7   Once the knots are baked, remove them from the oven and let them cool slightly. Toss the knots in melted garlic butter, making sure each piece is coated well. Place onto a serving plate and sprinkle with parmesan. Serve immediately.

Triple-cooked Fries

Everyone loves French fries, and these are the crème de la crème!
Make these for your friends, or just for yourself.

SERVES 4
PREP TIME 20 minutes plus drying
and cooling time
COOK TIME 25 minutes

4 large starchy potatoes (such as
brushed or golden delights)
vegetable oil, to deep-fry (see tip
below)
garlic aïoli, to serve

Other good frying oils include
peanut oil or beef tallow.

1. Peel the potatoes (or not – this is optional) and cut them into evenly-sized fries, about 2 cm thick. Rinse in cold water to remove excess starch.

2. Place into a large pot and cover with cold water. Add a pinch of salt and bring to the boil. Cook for about 8–10 minutes, or until they're very soft and almost falling apart (this ensures a fluffy interior). Drain well then lay them out on a baking tray lined with paper towel to dry completely.

3. Half-fill a large pot or deep-fryer with oil and heat to 150°C. Carefully fry the potatoes in batches for 3–4 minutes each batch, to cook them through without browning. This step gives the fries a soft, tender inside. Use a large slotted spoon to transfer to a baking tray lined with paper towels to drain. Set aside to cool for at least 30 minutes, or refrigerate for faster cooling.

4. Reheat the oil to 190°C. Fry the potatoes in batches again for 2–3 minutes each, or until golden brown and crispy. Drain well on clean paper towel.

5. Immediately season the fries with salt to taste. Serve hot, with a side of garlic aïoli.

Steak Taco with Pickled Onion and Goat's Cheese

Succulent, spiced beef, tangy pickled onions paired with creamy avocado and goat's cheese. This is the type of recipe that will leave you wishing for leftovers. They are simple enough to make any day of the week and are a perfect example of how much difference a little extra effort can make.

SERVES 4
PREP TIME 15 minutes plus 2 hours marinating
COOK TIME 15 minutes

500 g skirt steak
1 teaspoon paprika
½ teaspoon ground cumin
½ teaspoon ground coriander
½ teaspoon onion powder
½ teaspoon garlic powder
1 teaspoon dried oregano
1 teaspoon salt
½ teaspoon white pepper
1 tablespoon olive oil
1 tablespoon lemon juice
1 avocado
juice of ½ lime
avocado oil, for cooking
12 small flour tortillas

TO SERVE
pickled red onion
marinated goat's cheese
coriander leaves

1 Pat the steak dry with paper towel. Combine the paprika, cumin, coriander, onion powder, garlic powder, dried oregano, salt, pepper, olive oil and lemon juice. Rub all over the steak. Cover and leave to marinate in the fridge for at least 2 hours.

2 Close to serving time, mash the avocado in a bowl with the lime juice and a generous pinch of salt.

3 Heat a large cast-iron frying pan over medium-high heat until very hot. Add a small amount of avocado oil and swirl to coat the pan. Cook the steak for about 2-3 minutes each side, making sure to get a good sear on the outside, until the internal temperature reaches at least 55°C. Remove from the pan and let rest on a plate, covered with foil, for 10 minutes.

4 Meanwhile, heat up tortillas in a frying pan or the microwave (if you're lame).

5 Cut the steak into cubes. Place all the ingredients to serve onto the table.

6 To assemble the taco, smear some guacamole onto a tortilla, then add steak followed by some pickled red onion, marinated goat's cheese and coriander leaves.

Skirt steak is also known as flank steak. You probably won't find it at the supermarket, so ask your butcher. I think it's a perfect cut to use for tacos like these because it's relatively cheap and has a strong beef flavour.

Steak Fajita Quesadilla

This is one of my favourite mid-week meals. The thought of coming home to something fresh, hot and delicious always makes the day better. It's also a perfect way to use up leftover steak (if there ever is any).

SERVES 4
PREP TIME 15 minutes plus 2 hours marinating
COOK TIME 30 minutes

500 g skirt steak
3 tablespoons fajita seasoning (page 182), plus 2 tablespoons extra
1 tablespoon olive oil
juice of 1 lime
1 of each: small green, red and yellow capsicums, cut into thin strips
1 small brown onion, halved and cut into thin slices
2 cloves garlic, crushed
avocado oil, for cooking
4 large tortillas
coriander leaves
200 g mozzarella, grated
lime wedges, to serve

Avocado oil has a high smoke point, meaning it won't burn and give your food a burnt flavour. Other high smoke point oils/fats include peanut oil, grape seed oil and canola oil.

1   Pat the steak dry with paper towel and place into a shallow dish. Combine the 3 tablespoons fajita seasoning, olive oil and lime juice and drizzle all over the steak, turning to coat. Cover and leave to marinate in the fridge for at least 2 hours, or overnight for best results.

2   Place the capsicums and onion into a bowl. Add the extra fajita seasoning, garlic and a good pinch of salt. Toss to evenly coat in the seasoning

3   Heat a large cast-iron pan (or the barbecue) over medium-high heat. Add a little cooking oil and swirl to coat the pan. Place the steak into the pan and press down with a spatula to ensure even contact with the heat. Cook for 2–3 minutes each side or until the internal temperature reaches 55°C. Remove from the pan and let rest on a plate, covered with foil, for 10 minutes.

4   If the pan is relatively dry add a little more oil before chucking in the seasoned vegetables, making sure to drain any excess liquid first. Toss the vegetables around the pan to break up any fond (the brown bits on the bottom of the pan) left by the steak. Stirring constantly, cook the vegetables for 3–5 minutes or until the onions begin to turn translucent. If you aren't a fan of slightly crunchy veg, cook them a little longer.

5   Once the steak has rested and the vegetables are cooked slice the steak into thin strips across the grain of the meat. Flank steak can be very stringy, so we are helping our teeth out by doing this.

6   Heat a medium non-stick frying pan over medium heat. Lay a tortilla in the pan. Layer the cooked vegetables and sliced steak on one half of the tortilla. Top with coriander leaves and as much mozzarella as you would like (I just had to put a number next to it). Fold the empty side over the top. Gently toast the bottom side of the tortilla until golden brown, lifting with a spatula to have a peek then flip over to toast the other side and melt the cheese. This should take 2–3 minutes each side.

7   Repeat with remaining tortillas and filling. Serve with a squeeze of lime juice.

Breakfast Burrito

If breakfast is the most important meal of the day, why not also make it the most delicious.
I have made this on so many slow Sunday mornings and it never fails to impress.
These also freeze well so you can make multiple in advance for breakfast on the go.

SERVES 1
PREP TIME 10 minutes
COOK TIME 30 minutes

1 small washed potato,
   cut into small cubes
3 slices streaky bacon
3 eggs
15 g butter
30 cm flour tortilla
½ avocado, sliced
handful of baby spinach leaves
1 tablespoon barbecue sauce
50 g mozzarella, grated

SEASONING
¼ teaspoon garlic powder
¼ teaspoon onion powder
¼ teaspoon paprika
¼ teaspoon dried oregano
¼ teaspoon white pepper
¼ teaspoon salt

1. Preheat the oven to 200°C. Toss the potato with the seasoning ingredients until evenly coated. Spread onto a baking tray and roast for 20–25 minutes, flipping once halfway, until golden and crispy.

2. Meanwhile, line a baking tray with baking paper. Lay the bacon on the prepared tray and bake for 12 minutes, or until crispy and golden. Transfer to paper towel to drain and cool, then break into pieces.

3. While the bacon and potatoes are cooking, lightly beat the eggs in a bowl. Season with a pinch of salt and white pepper. In a small pan, melt the butter over medium-low heat. Add the egg and cook gently, stirring and folding often, until just set to a soft, creamy texture (avoid overcooking). Remove from heat and set aside.

4. Microwave the tortilla for 10–15 seconds to soften it and allow it to stretch. Lay out on a work surface. Layer the scrambled egg, crispy bacon, roast potato, avocado and baby spinach in the centre of the tortilla. Drizzle with barbecue sauce and season with a sprinkle of garlic powder, onion powder, paprika and oregano for extra flavour.

5. Lift the bottom edge of the tortilla over the filling, wrap it under and pull back towards yourself gently to create some tension. Next, carefully fold in the sides of the tortilla and then roll it up tightly, enclosing the filling.

6. Heat a large non-stick frying pan over medium-low heat. Spread the cheese over the base of the pan to create a thin layer with no gaps. When the cheese has fully melted and is starting to release some oils, lay the rolled burrito down in the centre of the cheese and roll it to one side to make the cheese stick. Roll it to the other side to stick all of the cheese to the outside of the burrito.

7. Slice the burrito in half and serve immediately.

TIP!

If you like, you can cook the potato in a preheated air fryer for 15–18 minutes, shaking the basket halfway through, until the potatoes are golden and crispy.

Gringo
Taco
Night

Gringo Taco Night

Personally, I don't have any problem with even the most basic taco night, but a little extra effort goes a long way. Cook this for your next taco night and you'll have everyone convinced you just got back from Mexico (not really, the tacos are pretty good though). This recipe is intended to be set out across the table so that everyone can make their own tacos, their way.

SERVES 3–4 (12 tacos)
PREP TIME 30 minutes
COOK TIME 35 minutes

12 flour tortillas or hard taco shells
guacamole (page 10)
300 ml sour cream
450 g cheddar cheese, grated
1 small iceberg lettuce, shredded

CORN AND BLACK BEAN SALSA
1–2 corn cobs, or ½ cup frozen corn
    kernels
2 tablespoons olive oil
200 g black beans, drained and
    rinsed
¼ red onion, finely diced
½ small yellow capsicum, diced
2 tablespoons thinly sliced
    coriander leaves
juice of ½ lime
¼ teaspoon ground cumin

PICO DE GALLO
5 Roma tomatoes, deseeded and
    diced
½ small red onion, finely diced
¼ cup coriander leaves, finely sliced
1 teaspoon olive oil
juice of ¼ lime (about 2 teaspoons)

1 To make the corn and black bean salsa, if using fresh corn, cut the kernels off the cobs. If using frozen corn, place into a sieve and run under cold water to thaw. Heat 1 tablespoon of the olive oil in a frying pan over medium-high heat. Add the fresh corn (skip this if using frozen corn) and sauté for about 3 minutes, until the corn is lightly charred. In a large bowl, combine the charred corn, black beans, onion, capsicum, coriander and lime juice. Stir in the remaining olive oil and ground cumin, and season with salt and freshly ground black pepper to taste. Let sit for 10 minutes for the flavors to get to know each other.

2 For the pico di gallo, combine the tomato, onion and coriander in a bowl. Add the olive oil and lime juice. Season with salt and freshly ground black pepper to taste. Stir to combine then set aside.

3 For the spiced beef, heat the oil in a large frying pan over medium-high heat. Add the beef and brown well, breaking it up with a spoon as it cooks. Remove the beef from the pan and set aside. In the same pan, add a little more oil if needed and sweat the onion and jalapeños with a small pinch of salt for 3–4 minutes, until soft. Add the garlic, chipotle chilli, paprika, cumin, oregano, salt and pepper. Cook, stirring, for about 30 seconds, until fragrant. Return the browned beef to the pan. Add the stock and coriander stems. Bring to a simmer, then reduce the heat to medium-low. Simmer, stirring occasionally, for 10–15 minutes, until thickened and the sauce clings to the beef. Add the lime juice, then taste and adjust seasoning as needed. Set aside.

SPICED BEEF

2 teaspoons olive oil, plus more if
    needed
1 kg lean beef mince
1 small brown onion, finely diced
2 jalapeños, seeds removed and
    finely diced
1 clove garlic, grated
2 tablespoons chipotle chilli in
    adobo sauce, chopped
2 tablespoons smoked paprika
1 tablespoon ground cumin
1 tablespoon dried oregano
1 teaspoon salt
½ teaspoon fresh cracked black
    pepper
400 ml beef stock
1 bunch fresh coriander stems, thinly
    sliced
juice of ½ lime

4   Heat the tortillas or taco shells in the oven or on a pan until warm (about
    5–7 minutes in a 180°C oven or 1–2 minutes per side in a hot pan for the
    tortillas).

5   You can build your taco however you want, but this is how I build mine.
    Spread a layer of guac in the centre of a warmed tortilla. Add a strip
    of sour cream on top of that, a few spoonfuls of spiced mince, grated
    cheese and a little of both the pico de gallo and corn and black bean
    salsa. Fill any extra space with shredded lettuce.

If you're making the salsa ahead
of time, prepare the base and let
it marinate in the fridge. Hold off
on adding delicate ingredients like
fresh herbs until just before serving.
This keeps them fresh, vibrant and
prevents them from getting mushy
or discoloured.

Barbecue Beef and Bacon Burger

Barbecue beef and bacon burger might just be the best use of alliteration in the English language – it rolls perfectly off the tongue the same way this burger will roll right past yours. I love a good burger and this is, in my opinion, a great burger. I know it says cook time of 1 hour, but that is mainly for the bacon onion jam, so make that in advance when you have spare time, then you will be able to throw this together pretty quickly.

SERVES 1
PREP TIME 20 minutes
COOK TIME 1 hour

3 slices streaky bacon
250 g beef mince
2 slices American cheddar cheese
1 sesame seed brioche bun, halved
   and lightly toasted
1 tablespoon barbecue sauce,
   or to taste
French fries, to serve
   (optional, page 17)

BACON ONION JAM
200 g streaky bacon, diced
3 large brown onions, thinly sliced
2 teaspoons salt
1 cup (220 g) brown sugar
2 tablespoons balsamic vinegar
2 tablespoons Worcestershire sauce

Bacon onion jam can be stored in the fridge for up to 1 week, or frozen for up to 2 months.

1. To make the bacon onion jam, place the bacon in a large frying pan over low heat. Cook for 10–20 minutes, stirring occasionally, to let the bacon render out its fat and become crispy. Remove the bacon from the pan and set aside, leaving as much fat as possible in the pan.

2. Add the onion and salt to the bacon fat. Cook over low heat, stirring occasionally, for 20–40 minutes, until the onions are deeply caramelised and very soft. If the onion begins to stick to the pan, deglaze with a small splash of water and continue cooking until the water evaporates.

3. Stir in the sugar, vinegar and Worcestershire sauce. Cook over medium heat for another 5–10 minutes, until the mixture thickens and the sugar caramelises.

4. Stir in the crispy bacon pieces. Taste and adjust the seasoning to your liking. Let the jam cool to room temperature, and store it in the fridge until you're ready to use it.

5. Preheat the oven to 200°C and line a baking tray with baking paper. Lay the bacon onto the prepared tray and bake for about 12 minutes or until crispy. Set aside.

6. Divide the beef mince into two equal portions, shaping each into a loose ball (don't overwork the meat). Heat a large cast-iron frying pan over medium-high heat until very hot. Place one beef ball into the pan and immediately smash it flat using a spatula or a heavy object (like another pan) to create a thin patty. Season generously with salt. After about 2 minutes, flip the patty and immediately place a slice of cheese on top. Cook for an additional 1–2 minutes until the cheese has melted and the patty is fully cooked. Transfer to a plate, and repeat with the second patty.

7. Spread barbecue sauce on the bottom half of the bun. Place both beef patties on top followed by the slices of crispy bacon. Add a spoonful of bacon onion jam, then top with the other half of the brioche bun.

8. Serve with a side of French fries or eat it as is.

Crispy Pork Belly Burger with Apple Slaw

I'm a lazy cook and most of the time I will make the simple option, but not this time.
The effort that goes into this burger is most definitely worth it: soft pork belly with crunchy
crackling, crisp and fresh slaw with a creamy, spicy mayonnaise all on a toasted bun –
it's unreal. I suggest making the buns from the Everything Dough (page 3) for these.

MAKES 3–4 burgers
PREP TIME 20 minutes plus
   overnight refrigeration
COOK TIME 1 hour 10 minutes

3–4 burger buns, halved and
   lightly toasted

PORK BELLY
600 g pork belly, skin on
½ cup (150 g) salt
1 tablespoon ground cumin
1 tablespoon ground coriander
1 tablespoon chilli powder

APPLE SLAW
2 cups (160 g) thinly sliced green
   cabbage
½ green apple, peeled and sliced
   into batons
¼ carrot, peeled and sliced into thin
   batons (or grated)
¼ cup (30 g) thinly sliced fennel
1 spring onion (green part only),
   thinly sliced
½ cup (150 g) mayonnaise
2 tablespoons apple cider vinegar
1 tablespoon onion powder
1 tablespoon garlic powder
1 teaspoon salt
1 teaspoon white pepper

CUCUMBER
1 Lebanese cucumber, peeled
1 tablespoon lemon juice

CHILLI MAYO SAUCE
½ cup (150 g) mayonnaise
2 tablespoons chilli oil (use your
   favourite)

1 To prepare the pork belly, pat the skin dry with paper towel. Using a sharp knife, score the skin of the pork belly in a diamond pattern, being careful not to cut into the fat. Cover the skin only with salt and place skin side up on a tray. Refrigerate overnight to allow the skin to dry out.

2 Preheat the oven to 180°C. Wipe away all the salt from the pork skin. Season the meat side of the pork belly with cumin, coriander and chilli powder. Place the pork belly on a wire rack set over a rimmed baking tray, skin side up. Roast for 1 hour, then increase the temperature to 220°C and roast for an additional 10 minutes to crisp up the skin. Set aside to cool slightly before slicing the pork belly into 3–4 portions, each with a nice piece of crispy crackling.

3 For the apple slaw, combine the cabbage, apple, carrot, fennel and spring onion in a mixing bowl. Add the mayonnaise, vinegar, onion powder, garlic powder, salt and white pepper. Stir to fully combine. Refrigerate for 15–30 minutes to allow the flavours to meld.

4 For the cucumber, using the veggie peeler, create thin ribbons of cucumber, and discard the seeds. Place the cucumber ribbons in a bowl, add the lemon juice and a pinch of salt, and toss to combine. Let sit in the fridge for 15 minutes. After this time, drain any excess liquid, leaving only the cucumber ribbons.

5 To make the chilli mayo sauce, combine the mayonnaise and chilli oil in a small bowl. Stir well to combine.

6 Spread a generous layer of chilli mayo on the bottom half of each toasted bun. Layer the cucumber ribbons on top of the mayo. Add 3–4 slices of crispy pork belly, ensuring some crackling is included with each slice. Top with a good amount of the apple slaw. Spread another layer of chilli mayo on the top bun and place it on top of the assembled burger.

Steak Frites Sando

There are a few flavour combinations that I think are 'perfect' – steak and chimichurri is one of them. Add that to a sandwich with crispy fries, cheese and mayo and it just gets better. This is a very messy sandwich but that's part of the experience. Don't forget paper towels.

SERVES 2
PREP TIME 15 minutes
COOK TIME 25–30 minutes

2 cups (150–180g) frozen shoestring
   fries

STEAK SANDWICH
300 g scotch fillet, at room
   temperature
¼ cup (60 ml) vegetable or canola oil
2 white bread rolls (sourdough,
   focaccia, or baguette)
2 tablespoons Kewpie mayo
4 slices pepper cheddar cheese
   (or regular cheddar)
½ bunch chives, sliced finely
1 cup rocket leaves

CHIMICHURRI
1 cup (packed) flat-leaf parsley
   leaves
½ cup oregano leaves
   (or 2 tablespoons dried oregano)
4 cloves garlic, peeled
2 tablespoons red wine vinegar
¼ cup (60 ml) olive oil
1 teaspoon dried chilli flakes,
   or to taste

1. To make the chimichurri, place the ingredients into a food processor and process until finely chopped and well combined. Season with salt and pepper to taste. Set aside.

2. Cook the frozen shoestring fries according to the package instructions, whether in a deep-fryer, air-fryer, or oven. Once cooked, immediately season with salt.

3. Meanwhile, for the steak sandwich, pat the steak dry with paper towels and season both sides liberally with salt.

4. Heat a cast-iron or stainless steel pan over medium-high heat until hot. (Test by dropping a small amount of water onto the pan; it should glide around the pan and not evaporate instantly.) Add enough vegetable or canola oil to cover the bottom of the pan. Place the steak in the pan and press it down with a heavy object (like a Chebbo's or Andy Cooks protein press – Google it!) to ensure that an even golden crust will form. Sear the steak for 2–3 minutes on each side, until the internal temperature reaches 40°C. Remove the steak from the pan and set aside to rest for at least 10 minutes.

5. Preheat the oven to 180°C. Place the bread into the oven for 3–6 minutes, uncut, until the outside is crisp and golden while the inside remains soft. Cut each loaf in half horizontally. Scoop out some of the inside of the bread to create space for the fillings.

6. Slice the rested steak against the grain into thin strips. Spread a generous layer of mayo on the bottom half of each loaf. Layer with the sliced steak, followed by the cheese slices (melted with a kitchen torch or under a grill until bubbling and golden). Add the crispy fries, chives, a generous drizzle of chimichurri and a handful of rocket leaves. Place the top half of the bread roll on top.

7. Slice the sandwich through the centre and serve immediately.

If the steak is in the fridge and you are short on time, place the steak in an airtight bag and submerge it in warm (slightly above room temperature) water for 10–15 minutes.

Chicken Parmi Sandwich

Yeah, it's called a parmi. If you call it a parma I don't want to see you eating this sandwich.
Just kidding, call it what you want because I know what you'll be calling me after you eat this.

SERVES 2
PREP TIME 20 minutes
COOK TIME 40 minutes

SCHNITZEL
1 large chicken breast fillet,
    sliced in 2 horizontally
1 cup (75 g) panko breadcrumbs
¼ cup flat-leaf parsley leaves,
    finely chopped
1 teaspoon garlic powder
1 teaspoon onion powder
1 teaspoon salt
1 teaspoon white pepper
1 cup (150 g) plain flour
1 egg
olive oil, to shallow-fry

PARMI SAUCE
2 tablespoons olive oil
2 cloves garlic, crushed
1 teaspoon dried chilli flakes
    (optional – if you like spice)
400 g can cherry tomatoes
1 teaspoon dried oregano
1 teaspoon dried basil
1 teaspoon dried thyme
1 teaspoon dried rosemary
1 teaspoon white sugar
1 teaspoon white pepper

SANDWICH
2 long white rolls, about 150 g each
2–4 slices prosciutto (or ham if
    preferred)
50–100 g fresh mozzarella, sliced
2 tablespoons basil pesto (page 202)

1   For the schnitzel, pat the chicken dry with paper towels. Season both sides lightly with salt and pepper. In a blender or food processor, combine the panko breadcrumbs, parsley, garlic powder, onion powder, salt and white pepper. Blend until fully combined then transfer to a shallow bowl. Place the flour into a separate shallow bowl, and lightly beat the egg in a third bowl. Dredge each piece of chicken in the flour, ensuring it's fully coated. Dip it into the beaten egg, allowing any excess to drip off. Next, coat the chicken in the seasoned breadcrumbs, pressing down gently to ensure they stick. Set the coated chicken aside on a plate.

2   To make the parmi sauce, heat the olive oil in a small saucepan over medium heat. Add the garlic and chilli flakes and cook briefly until fragrant (be careful not to burn the garlic). Add the canned tomatoes (be cautious as the oil may splatter) and stir to combine. Bring the sauce to a simmer. Stir in the herbs, sugar and white pepper. Simmer for 15–25 minutes, or until thickened enough to coat the back of a spoon. If desired, blend the sauce with a stick blender for a smoother texture, though the chunkier sauce works well for a sandwich. Taste and adjust the seasoning with salt as needed. Remove from heat and set aside to cool slightly.

3   Add enough olive oil to coat the bottom of a large frying pan 1cm deep and heat over medium heat. Add the chicken and shallow fry for 3–4 minutes per side, or until golden brown and fully cooked through (internal temperature should reach 75°C). Remove the chicken from the pan and drain on a plate lined with paper towel, or a wire rack set over a baking tray.

4   Preheat the oven to 180°C.

5   Slice the bread rolls open lengthwise and place them on a baking tray lined with baking paper. Spread a layer of Parmi sauce on the bottom side of each roll. Top with chicken, then add more sauce, followed by a few slices of prosciutto (or ham, if you're a loser) and slices of fresh mozzarella. Bake for 5–8 minutes, or until the mozzarella is melted and slightly browned on top. Remove roll tops once toasted and browned.

6   Spread basil pesto on the top side of the roll and place over the bottom half. Serve immediately.

One-can Pizza Sauce

This pizza sauce is perfect for cooking at higher heats for a shorter time because it has a higher moisture content (the higher heat will evaporate the moisture and concentrate the flavour). A punchy and fresh tomato base for your homemade pizzas. You can make it in 5 minutes and in the same can the tomatoes come in: it's a win-win.

SERVES 6–8 (2 tablespoons per serving)
PREP TIME 5 minutes

400 g can Italian diced tomatoes
1 clove garlic, crushed
1 teaspoon dried oregano
1 teaspoon dried basil
1 teaspoon onion powder
1 teaspoon garlic powder
1 teaspoon dried thyme
1 teaspoon salt
1 teaspoon chilli flakes (optional)

1. Combine all the ingredients in a mixing bowl.

2. Use a stick blender to blend the mixture until smooth. If you don't have a stick blender, you can transfer the mixture to a regular blender and blend until smooth.

3. Transfer the sauce to an airtight container and store in the fridge.

4. When ready to serve, scoop out about 2 tablespoons per serving and spread over your prepared pizza base.

Keep in the fridge for up to 1 week, or freeze in serving portions for up to 3 months.

Chilli
Prawn
Pizza

Chilli Prawn Pizza

Whenever I'm asked what my favourite food is, 99 per cent of the time I'm saying pizza. Specifically Neapolitan pizza. I love the simplicity of it and the comparison in time taking hours or days to make the dough but then only taking 2 minutes to bake it. A chilli prawn pizza was the first time I tried Neapolitan-style pizza and this recipe is my closest recreation to how that tasted.

SERVES 2
PREP TIME 10 minutes
COOK TIME 8–10 minutes

200 g Everything Dough (page 3)
2 tablespoons One-can Pizza Sauce
   (page 36)
8 uncooked prawns, peeled and
   deveined
70 g fresh mozzarella, torn into
   rough pieces
1 tablespoon chilli oil (or to taste)
   (page 186)
½ cup rocket leaves
1 tablespoon finely grated parmesan
1 teaspoon extra virgin olive oil

If using homemade dough, stretch or roll out the 200 g pizza dough into a 25–30 cm round shape on a lightly floured surface. Transfer the rolled dough to a parchment paper or pizza peel if you're using a pizza oven, or directly onto a pizza stone or steel if using a regular oven.

1 Preheat the oven to 250°C, placing a pizza stone or steel inside to heat up for at least 30 minutes. If you have a pizza oven, preheat to 450°C or follow the manufacturer's instructions for temperature.

2 Stretch or roll out the dough on a lightly floured surface to a 25–30 cm round. Transfer the rolled dough directly onto the preheated pizza stone or steel, or if you're using a pizza oven, place onto a pizza peel.

3 Spread the sauce evenly over the surface of the dough, leaving about a 1–2 cm border around the edges for the crust.

4 Season the prawns lightly with salt, then arrange them evenly on top of the sauce. Place the mozzarella in the gaps between the prawns, spreading it out evenly across the pizza. Drizzle with chilli oil.

5 Slide the pizza onto the preheated pizza stone or steel in your oven. Bake for 8–10 minutes, or until the crust is golden and crispy, and the prawns are cooked through (they should be pink and opaque). To cook in a pizza oven, place the pizza directly onto the pizza stone or floor of the pizza oven. Bake for 4–6 minutes, or until the crust is golden, the prawns are cooked, and the cheese is bubbling and melted.

6 Remove pizza from the oven. Top with a handful of rocket leaves and sprinkle with parmesan. Finish with a drizzle of extra virgin olive oil for added richness. Slice the pizza into wedges and serve immediately, enjoying the fresh contrast of spicy prawns, creamy mozzarella and peppery rocket.

Four Cheese Calzone

A calzone is what I think about when I hear New Yorkers say 'Lemme get
a pizza pie'. This giant hot pocket filled with melty cheese is the perfect
handheld meal or if you think you're fancy you could use a knife and fork.

SERVES 1 large calzone
PREP TIME 10 minutes
COOK TIME 10–15 minutes

200 g Everything Dough (page 3)
2 tablespoons One-can Pizza Sauce
   (page 36)
30 g mozzarella, grated
30 g cheddar cheese, grated
20 g finely grated parmesan
20 g gorgonzola, crumbled
olive oil, for brushing
½ teaspoon dried oregano (optional)
½ teaspoon garlic powder (optional)
extra pizza sauce, for dipping
   (optional)

1. Preheat the oven to 250°C, placing a pizza stone or steel inside to heat up for at least 30 minutes. If you have a pizza oven, preheat to 450°C or follow the manufacturer's instructions for temperature.

2. On a lightly floured surface, roll out the dough to a 25–30 cm round. You want it to be thin but not so thin that it will tear when folded. Spread the pizza sauce evenly across one half of the dough, leaving about a 2–3 cm border around the edges. Sprinkle the cheeses over the pizza sauce, spreading them out evenly.

3. Carefully fold the plain side of the dough over the filling to create a half-moon shape, ensuring the edges align. Gently press down to seal the edges. Use a fork to crimp the edges, pressing down around the border to ensure it's tightly sealed and prevent any filling from spilling out during baking. Use a sharp knife to make a 2–3 small slits in the top of the calzone to allow steam to escape while baking. This will help it cook evenly and prevent it from bursting.

4. Brush the top of the calzone lightly with olive oil for a golden, crispy crust. You can also sprinkle the top with dried oregano or garlic powder for extra flavour if you like. Place the calzone directly onto the preheated pizza stone or steel in the oven (or on a baking tray if you don't have one). Bake for 10–15 minutes, or until the crust is golden brown and the cheese inside has melted.

5. To cook in a pizza oven, slide the calzone onto the preheated pizza stone or the pizza oven floor. Bake for about 5–7 minutes, checking occasionally for golden brown colour.

6. Remove the calzone from the oven and let it rest for 2–3 minutes to allow the cheese to cool slightly. Cut into wedges and serve while melty! Serve the calzone with extra pizza sauce for dipping.

CHAPTER 2

(Almost) One Pan Wonders

Rigatoni Vodka Pasta

This recipe was 100 per cent going in the book! I can't tell you how many times I've eaten this exact same pasta dish and it never gets old. This is one of my most successful videos online to this day, with over 10 MILLION views!! If you haven't tried it yet, you're in for an absolute treat.

SERVES 2–3
PREP TIME 10 minutes
COOK TIME about 20 minutes

250 g rigatoni
1 tablespoon olive oil
100 g pancetta, diced
2 golden shallots, finely diced
2 cloves garlic, finely diced
1 teaspoon dried chilli flakes
1 teaspoon oregano
60 g tomato paste
1 shot vodka (about 30 ml)
1 cup (250 ml) thickened cream
80 g finely grated parmesan,
    plus extra for serving
flat-leaf parsley, chopped

1 Bring a large pot of salted water to a boil. Add the rigatoni and cook according to package instructions (usually 10–12 minutes) until al dente. Reserve about 1 cup pasta cooking water before draining.

2 While the pasta is cooking, heat oil in a large frying pan over medium heat. Add the diced pancetta and cook for 5–6 minutes, stirring occasionally, until crispy and golden. Remove the pancetta and set aside.

3 In the same pan, add the shallots and cook for 2–3 minutes, until softened and translucent. Add the garlic, chilli flakes and oregano, and cook for another 1–2 minutes until fragrant.

4 Stir in the tomato paste and cook for 2 minutes, allowing the paste to caramelise and deepen in flavour.

5 Add the shot of vodka to the pan, stirring to deglaze. Let the vodka cook off for 1–2 minutes, until the alcohol has evaporated.

6 Reduce the heat to low and stir in the cream. Mix until the sauce becomes smooth and creamy. Allow the sauce to simmer gently for 3–4 minutes to thicken slightly. Add salt and pepper to taste.

7 Add the drained rigatoni to the pan with the sauce. If the sauce seems too thick, add a little reserved pasta cooking water, a tablespoon at a time, until you reach your desired consistency. Stir in the parmesan, mixing until it's fully incorporated and the sauce becomes creamy and glossy.

8 Stir the crispy pancetta into the pasta and sauce. Sprinkle with parsley and extra parmesan, and serve immediately.

Super Cheesy Chorizo Pasta

This recipe has all of my favourite food groups – pasta, cheese and chorizo. The spicy chorizo is balanced with the cream and the cheese does what cheese does, makes everything better. Cheesy chorizo pasta is perfect for a weeknight meal, a weekend meal or even a midnight 'snack'.

SERVES 2–3
PREP TIME 10 minutes
COOK TIME about 20 minutes

250 g curly fettuccine or conchiglie
2 spicy fresh chorizo sausages
olive oil, to drizzle
2 cloves garlic, crushed
210 g can chopped tomatoes
⅓ cup (80 ml) thickened cream
200 g shredded mozzarella

The flavour for this meal comes from good quality chorizo. If you can't get your hands on some, simply add 1 tablespoon of cumin and 1 tablespoon of smoky paprika.

1. Bring a pot of salted water to a boil. Add the pasta and cook according to the package instructions (usually 9–11 minutes) until al dente. Drain the pasta, reserving about ½ cup of the pasta cooking water.

2. Meanwhile, remove the casings from the chorizo and crumble the sausage into pieces. Heat a frying pan over medium heat and add a small drizzle of olive oil. Add the crumbled chorizo to the pan and cook for 5 minutes, using a wooden spoon to break the sausage apart and allow it to render out its fat and get some colour.

3. Add the garlic to the pan and stir for 1 minute, to allow the garlic to cook without burning. Pour in the tomatoes and cook for 10 minutes, allowing the sauce to simmer and thicken slightly.

4. Add the drained pasta into the tomato mixture. Stir well to combine. If the sauce is too thick, add a bit of the reserved pasta cooking water to achieve the desired consistency.

5. Pour in the cream and stir until the sauce becomes smooth and creamy. Turn off the heat and add the mozzarella. Stir until the cheese melts into the sauce, creating a luscious, cheesy coating for the pasta.

6. Taste the dish and adjust the seasoning with salt and pepper to your liking. Divide among plates and serve immediately, topped with additional cheese if desired.

Spaghetti Aglio e Olio

When I was younger my mum would make this for us as a quick dinner that really takes no effort at all. Then my sister started cooking it for us and I decided that I needed to learn to make it too. Even though this recipe is so simple, it teaches you how to infuse flavour into the oil, which is the main pillar of flavour in this dish, and also how to emulsify your 'sauce' with the starchy cooking water from the spaghetti. Once you can nail this dish, you'll be able to cook anything.

SERVES 2
PREP TIME 5 minutes
COOK TIME 15 minutes

½ cup (125 ml) extra virgin olive oil
4 cloves garlic, finely sliced
2 small red chillies (or to taste),
   finely sliced
200 g spaghetti
2 tablespoons finely chopped
   flat-leaf parsley
finely grated parmesan, to taste

1 Pour the olive oil into a large frying pan and set it over medium-low heat. Allow the oil to warm gently.

2 Add the garlic and chilli to the warm oil. Cook for 4–5 minutes, stirring occasionally, until the garlic has softened and is lightly golden. Be careful not to let it burn, as this can make the dish bitter.

3 Meanwhile, bring a large pot of salted water to a boil. Add the spaghetti and cook according to the package instructions (usually 8–10 minutes) until al dente.

4 Once the pasta is ready, reserve ⅓ cup pasta cooking water. Use tongs to transfer the spaghetti directly from the pot into the pan with the garlic and chilli-infused oil. Add ¼ cup of the pasta cooking water to the pan. Stir well, ensuring the pasta is fully coated in the oil mixture.

5 Continue stirring the pasta vigorously as the water begins to evaporate. The water will emulsify with the oil, forming a slightly thickened sauce. Keep stirring until the sauce is glossy and coats the pasta evenly.

6 Stir in the parsley and parmesan, mixing well to combine. Taste the dish and season with salt as needed.

7 If the sauce becomes too thick, add remaining pasta cooking water to loosen it up and help it coat the pasta more easily.

8 Divide the spaghetti between two plates, top with extra parmesan if desired, and serve immediately.

Spinach
and Ricotta
Stuffed
Shells

Spinach and Ricotta Stuffed Shells

This recipe is another viral one. I filmed this as part of my '20-minute recipes for 20 days' and even though this definitely didn't take me 20 minutes and I think I posted it on day 35 or something, it still stands as one of my favourite meals that I've cooked online. What I never told anyone was that when I was filming the video for this recipe, my frying pan didn't fit in my oven so I had to leave the door open and hope that the grill would finish cooking the pasta. It didn't – I just acted like the pasta wasn't still raw!

SERVES 4
PREP TIME 25 minutes
COOK TIME 35 minutes

2 tablespoons olive oil
100 g spinach, roughly chopped
6 cloves garlic, crushed
800 g can chopped tomatoes
1 teaspoon dried chilli flakes
1 teaspoon dried basil
1 teaspoon dried thyme
1 teaspoon dried oregano
200g large pasta shells
250 g smooth ricotta
1 egg
¼ cup (15 g) fresh breadcrumbs
  plus ¼ cup (15 g) for topping
50 g grated mozzarella
  plus 50 g for topping
20 g finely grated parmesan
  plus 20 g for topping

1   Preheat the oven to 180°C. Heat 1 tablespoon of the olive oil in a large ovenproof frying pan over medium heat. Add half the garlic and sauté for 1 minute before adding the spinach and a good pinch of salt. Sauté for 2–3 minutes to wilt and remove some moisture. Transfer to a large mixing bowl, then set aside to cool slightly and roughly chop.

2   Put the pan back on the heat and add the rest of the olive oil and garlic, cooking for 30 seconds, until aromatic.

3   Add the tomatoes, chilli, basil, thyme, oregano and a pinch of salt and sugar, stirring to combine. Turn the heat up to medium-high and bring to a simmer and cook for 10–15 minutes, until reduced and thickened slightly.

4   Meanwhile, cook the pasta shells in a large saucepan of well-salted boiling water until al dente. Pour into a mesh strainer and rinse under cold running water for 1 minute to stop cooking. Drain well.

5   Combine the ricotta, egg, spinach mixture, breadcrumbs, mozzarella and parmesan in a bowl. Stir well to combine and pipe or spoon into the cooked pasta shells.

6   Remove ⅔ of the sauce from the frying pan and set aside.

7   Arrange the stuffed shells in the pan. Cover with the reserved sauce and extra mozzarella, breadcrumbs and parmesan.

8   Bake for 15 minutes minutes for the filling and pasta shells to cook, turning the grill setting on for the final 1–2 mins of cooking to melt and crisp up the cheese.

F**k Me Chicken

Some people want to call it 'Marry me chicken' but I think once you eat this you'll be saying 'f**k me, that's good'. The first time I made this recipe was for my mates and they absolutely loved it, eating it straight out of the frying pan!

SERVES 4
PREP TIME 20 minutes
COOK TIME 30 minutes

⅔ cup (100g) plain flour
2 tablespoons garlic powder
4 teaspoons onion powder
2 teaspoons dried oregano
2 teaspoons dried thyme
2 teaspoons dried basil
1 tablespoon smoked paprika
2 teaspoons salt
2 teaspoons black pepper
2 chicken breast fillets, halved
  horizontally
50 g butter
1 tablespoon olive oil
3 cloves garlic, crushed
1 teaspoon dried chilli flakes
1½ cups (375 ml) chicken stock
1 cup (250 ml) thickened cream
½ cup flat-leaf parsley, chopped
250 g penne
40 g finely grated parmesan
¼ cup basil leaves, chopped

1 In a shallow bowl, whisk together the flour with half of the garlic powder, onion powder, dried oregano, thyme, basil, smoked paprika, salt and pepper. Mix until evenly combined.

2 Pat the chicken dry with paper towels. Coat both sides of each piece in the flour mixture, pressing gently to ensure an even coating. Set the coated chicken aside.

3 Heat a large saucepan over medium heat. Add the butter and olive oil, allowing the butter to melt and the oil to heat up for about 1 minute. Add half the chicken to the pan and cook for 3–4 minutes on each side, until golden brown and fully cooked through. Repeat with remaining chicken. Set aside.

4 Drain any excess fat from the pan, leaving about 1 tablespoon behind. Add the garlic and chilli flakes to the pan and sauté for 30 seconds, until fragrant. Pour in the chicken stock and cream, stirring to combine. Add the remaining dried oregano, thyme, dried basil, smoked paprika and onion powder. Bring the sauce to a gentle simmer and cook for about 10 minutes, stirring occasionally, until the sauce thickens slightly.

5 Return the chicken to the pan, turning over to coat evenly in the creamy sauce. Let the chicken simmer in the sauce for 5 minutes, to absorb the flavours while the sauce thickens.

6 Meanwhile, bring a large pot of salted water to the boil. Add the penne and cook according to package instructions (usually 9–11 minutes) until al dente. Drain the pasta, reserving a small cup of the pasta cooking water.

7 Remove the cooked chicken from the sauce and set aside. Add the cooked pasta to the saucepan with the creamy sauce. Toss the pasta in the sauce, adding a little reserved pasta water if necessary to help the sauce coat the pasta. Stir in the parmesan, parsley and basil.

8 Slice the cooked chicken into strips and serve it on top of the creamy pasta. Sprinkle with extra parmesan if desired. Serve immediately.

Rigatoni in Romesco Sauce

This light and creamy sauce is perfect for a simple pasta dish like this, but can also be used in a range of different ways like on grilled seafood, roasted vegetables or even just to dip a corn chip in. As a typical man I tend to steer away from a vegetarian recipe by adding some form of meat but this recipe was so flavourful that I ate it faster than you can say 'steak'.

SERVES 4
PREP TIME 15 minutes
COOK TIME 30 minutes

2 red capsicums, cut in half
4 tomatoes, halved
50 g almonds
1 slice day-old bread, crusts
    removed
2 cloves garlic
1 teaspoon salt
1 teaspoon dried chilli flakes
1 teaspoon paprika
1 tablespoon red wine vinegar
½ cup (125 ml) olive oil
400g rigatoni
chopped flat-leaf parsley and finely
    grated parmesan, to serve

1   Preheat the grill to high. Place the capsicum halves and tomatoes, cut side down, on a baking tray. Cook under the grill for 5–10 minutes, or until the skins are blackened and charred.

2   Remove the tray from the oven and immediately transfer the vegetables to a heatproof bowl. Cover the bowl tightly with plastic wrap and allow them to steam for 5 minutes. This will make peeling the skins easier.

3   While the vegetables are steaming, place the almonds in a dry frying pan over medium heat. Toast for 4–5 minutes, stirring occasionally, until they become fragrant. Remove from the pan and set aside to cool slightly.

4   Peel the charred skins from the vegetables. Remove the stems and seeds from the capsicum, and scoop the seeds out of the tomatoes. Place the peeled capsicum and tomatoes in a blender. Add the toasted almonds, bread, garlic, salt, chilli flakes, paprika and red wine vinegar.

5   Blend the mixture until smooth and combined, about 1 minute. With the motor running, slowly drizzle in the olive oil to emulsify and thicken the sauce. Taste and adjust seasoning if needed.

6   Bring a large pot of salted water to a boil. Add the rigatoni and cook according to package instructions (usually 9–11 minutes) until al dente. Reserve about ½ cup of pasta cooking water, then drain the pasta.

7   In a large frying pan, place the drained pasta over medium heat. Add about ½ of the romesco sauce, saving the rest to add on top at the end, plus ½ cup of the reserved pasta cooking water. Toss the pasta in the sauce, stirring frequently until it thickens and coats the pasta evenly.

8   Divide the pasta among serving plates. Top with parsley and a generous sprinkle of grated parmesan. Serve immediately.

Spicy Gochujang Pasta with Burrata

Before 2024 the only thing I knew about Korea was that Son Heung-min was the Spurs striker. Since the deserved spike in popularity Korean food has had online, I now know about gochujang (Korean fermented chilli paste) and how damn good it is. Gochujang has a slightly sweet and smoky flavour with a little spice – it's not as hot as sriracha sauce. This dish is a great combination of spicy and creamy but you can ramp it up by adding as much chilli oil as you want.

SERVES 2
PREP TIME 10 minutes
COOK TIME 20 minutes

250g fusilli
80 g unsalted butter, chopped
3 cloves garlic, crushed
3 tablespoons gochujang
1 cup (250 ml) thickened cream
1 fresh burrata (about 150 g)
chilli oil, to serve (page 186)

1   Bring a large pot of salted water to the boil. Add the pasta and stir for about 30 seconds to avoid it sticking together. Cook according to package instructions (usually 8 minutes) until al dente.

2   Meanwhile, heat a large frying pan over medium heat and add 50 g of the butter to melt. Once the butter is foamy add the garlic and stir constantly for 30 seconds, until fragrant. Garlic can burn very easily so don't walk away!!

3   Stir in the gochujang and cook for another 30 seconds or so. Cooking the gochujang can mellow its flavour, which is perfect if you don't deal well with spice, like me.

4   Once the oil from the gochujang turns red pour in the thickened cream and mix to incorporate. Keep stirring to avoid the cream burning on the pan. Bring just to a simmer and then reduce the heat to cook gently until the cream has reduced by roughly half. Reducing the cream too much can cause it to split and we want to avoid that.

5   When the pasta is 1–2 minutes from being fully cooked, use tongs to transfer it from the boiling water into the cream sauce, along with ⅔ cup of the pasta water. Increase the heat slightly to bring it all back to a simmer and stir constantly until the pasta is fully cooked and the sauce thickens. Add the remaining butter and swirl it through the sauce. This will emulsify and create a smooth, velvety sauce.

6   Remove from the heat and taste for seasoning. Add salt a little at a time to avoid over seasoning.

7   Transfer to a big serving dish and place the burrata in the centre. Break it open and drizzle with the chilli oil.

Hokkien
Noodle Beef
Stir Fry

Hokkien Noodle Beef Stir-fry

A stir-fry has it all – flavour, variety of texture, a balance of nutrition and it can be made so quickly and easily. Everyone knows that the best stir-fry is cooked in a wok by highly skilled chefs, but you can make it at home in a frying pan and no one needs to know. This is a perfect recipe for a midweek meal and it's great the next day for lunch. Even my girlfriend agrees.

SERVES 3–4
PREP TIME 15 minutes
COOK TIME 15 minutes

450 g fresh hokkein noodles
300 g steak (flank or sirloin), thinly
    sliced across the grain
2 tablespoons vegetable oil
2 cloves garlic, finely chopped
3 cm piece ginger, peeled and
    finely grated
1 small brown onion, thinly sliced
1 cup (80g) wombok (Chinese
    cabbage), thinly sliced
1 bunch bok choy, roughly chopped
coriander, spring onion and chilli oil
    (page 186), to serve (optional)

SAUCE
2 tablespoons regular soy sauce
1 tablespoon dark soy sauce
1 tablespoon oyster sauce
1 tablespoon hoisin sauce
1 teaspoon sesame oil
1 teaspoon cornflour
½ cup (125 ml) beef or vegetable
    stock (or water)

1. To make the sauce, mix the soy sauces, oyster sauce, hoisin sauce, sesame oil and cornflour with the stock or water in a small bowl. Set aside.

2. Bring a large pot of water to a boil. Add the hokkien noodles and cook according to package instructions (usually 2–3 minutes for fresh noodles). Drain and set aside.

3. Season the steak lightly with salt and pepper. Heat 1 tablespoon of the oil in a large frying pan or wok over medium-high heat. Add the beef to the pan in a single layer. Pan fry for 1–2 minutes, flipping half way, until browned and just cooked through. Remove the beef from the pan and set aside.

4. Heat the remaining oil in the same pan. Add the garlic and ginger, stir-frying for about 30 seconds, until fragrant. Add the onion and stir-fry for 2–3 minutes, until it is slightly translucent but still has some crunch. If you prefer fully cooked onion, cook for another 1–2 minutes.

5. Return the cooked beef to the pan along with the vegetables. Add the noodles and toss everything together. Pour the sauce over the beef and noodles, tossing everything to coat evenly. Stir-fry for 2–3 minutes, until the noodles are heated through and the sauce has thickened slightly.

6. Taste and adjust the seasoning with more soy sauce or salt if needed. Top with fresh coriander or spring onion if desired. If you want it to be spicy you can drizzle (or drown it) with homemade chilli oil (page 186).

Szechuan Chilli Garlic Prawns with Blistered Cherry Tomatoes

White people can't handle spice. I don't know if that's true for all of us but I know it is for me. One of the first times I tried Szechuan pepper was by accident. I was at a hotpot place and chose the sensible Caucasian option. I ordered the tomato soup base, but when it arrived it wasn't that. Instead, I was given the spiciest soup they had, with 5 floating red chillies and maybe 4 billion Szechuan peppercorns. I was crying, mouth burning and sweating like crazy. These chilli garlic prawns are nothing like that, meaning they are just a bit less spicy.

SERVES 2
PREP TIME 10 minutes
COOK TIME 20 minutes

1 tablespoon olive oil
1 teaspoon Szechuan peppercorns
2 cloves garlic, finely chopped
1 small golden shallot, finely chopped
1 teaspoon dried chilli flakes, or to taste
250 g punnet cherry tomatoes
250 g pasta (spaghetti, linguine or your choice)
200 g raw prawns, peeled and deveined
½ cup (15g) chopped flat-leaf parsley, plus extra for garnish
juice of ½ lemon
½ cup reserved pasta water
chilli oil (optional, page 186)

1 Heat the oil in a large frying pan over medium-low heat. Add the Szechuan peppercorns, garlic, shallot and dried chilli flakes. Cook gently for 2–3 minutes, stirring occasionally, until the shallots soften and the oil is infused with the flavours of the garlic and peppercorns. Be careful not to burn the garlic.

2 Increase the heat to medium-high. Add the whole cherry tomatoes to the pan and cook for about 5 minutes, stirring or gently shaking the pan occasionally. The tomatoes should start to blister and burst open, releasing their juices. Once they begin to split, use a spoon or a fork to gently crush them in the pan, releasing their pulp and creating a chunky sauce.

3 Meanwhile, bring a pot of salted water to a boil. Add the pasta and cook according to the package instructions (usually 9–11 minutes) until al dente. Reserve about ½ cup of pasta water before draining the pasta.

4 Season the prawns lightly with salt and add to the pan. Cook for 1–2 minutes on each side until they turn pink and are just cooked through. Remove the prawns from the pan and set aside.

5 Add the drained pasta directly into the pan with the blistered, crushed tomatoes. Pour in the reserved pasta water, a tablespoon at a time, while stirring vigorously to emulsify the sauce and make it creamy. Adjust with more pasta water if needed to achieve your desired sauce consistency.

6 Return the cooked prawns to the pan with the pasta. Add the parsley and lemon juice and stir everything together for 1–2 minutes to combine. This will infuse the dish with freshness and brightness.

7 Serve immediately, garnished with extra fresh parsley and a squeeze of lemon if desired. Drizzle with chilli oil to taste, if you like.

Szechuan Chilli Garlic Prawns

Penne Arrabbiata

Arrabbiata translates to 'angry' and I have no idea why. This rich and spicy pasta made me feel a lot of things but anger wasn't one of them. This is another recipe that you can make in little to no time and it packs an insane punch. I'm going to apologise to any nonna that may see this because it's probably not very traditional, sorry.

SERVES 3–4
PREP TIME 10 minutes
COOK TIME 20 minutes

300 g penne
2 tablespoons olive oil
3 garlic cloves, thinly sliced
1–2 teaspoons dried chilli flakes,
    or to taste
400 g can crushed tomatoes
chopped flat-leaf parsley and finely
    grated parmesan, to serve

1 Bring a large pot of salted water to a boil. Add the penne and cook according to the package instructions (usually about 10 minutes) until al dente. Reserve ½ cup of pasta cooking water, then drain the penne and set aside.

2 While the pasta is cooking, heat the olive oil in a large frying pan over medium heat. Add the garlic and cook for 1–2 minutes, stirring frequently, until it becomes fragrant and golden, but keep an eye on it because garlic can burn easily. Add the chilli flakes to the garlic and cook for an additional 30 seconds to release the flavour.

3 Pour in the crushed tomatoes and stir to combine. Season with a pinch of salt and pepper to taste. Let the sauce simmer for 10–12 minutes, stirring occasionally, until it thickens slightly.

4 Add the cooked penne to the sauce, tossing to coat the pasta evenly. If the sauce is too thick, add a little bit of the reserved pasta cooking water to loosen it up. Cook for another 1–2 minutes, allowing the pasta to absorb some of the sauce.

5 Taste and adjust the seasoning, adding more salt or chilli flakes if needed. Serve sprinkled with parsley and parmesan.

Fettuccine Boscaiola

'This isn't a carbonara!!!!' said the angry Italian. I feel like everyone should know by now that the Aussie carbonara really isn't carbonara at all, everyone except my dad who would make this at least once a week. He also would 'experiment' when it was his turn to cook and 80 per cent of the time it was a wild ride at dinner time. This recipe is one that he nailed every time.

SERVES 2
PREP TIME 10 minutes
COOK TIME 20 minutes

200 g fettuccine
1 tablespoon olive oil
200 g bacon, diced
1 tablespoon butter
1 golden shallot, finely diced
1 clove garlic, grated
200 g mushrooms, thinly sliced
½ cup (125 ml) white wine
200 ml thickened cream
¼ cup flat-leaf parsley, finely sliced
50 g finely grated parmesan, plus
    extra to serve

1   Bring a large pot of salted water to a boil. Cook the fettuccine according to package instructions (usually 8–10 minutes) until al dente. Reserve about ½ cup pasta cooking water, then drain and set aside.

2   While the pasta is cooking, heat the olive oil in a large frying pan over medium heat. Add the bacon and cook for 5–6 minutes, stirring occasionally, until the bacon is crispy and the fat has rendered out. Remove the bacon from the frying pan and set aside, leaving the rendered fat in the pan.

3   In the same pan, add the butter and heat until melted. Add the shallot and garlic and cook for 1–2 minutes, until soft and fragrant. Add the mushrooms and cook for another 5–6 minutes, stirring occasionally, until the mushrooms are golden and the moisture has evaporated.

4   Pour in the white wine, stirring to deglaze the pan. Let it simmer for 2–3 minutes to allow the alcohol to evaporate and the wine to reduce slightly. Add the thickened cream and stir to combine with the mushrooms and wine. Bring the sauce to a gentle simmer, cooking for 3–4 minutes, until it thickens slightly. Return the cooked bacon to the pan and stir everything together. Season with salt and pepper to taste.

5   Add the cooked fettuccine to the sauce, tossing gently to coat the pasta evenly. If the sauce is too thick, add some of the reserved pasta cooking water, a little at a time, until you reach your desired consistency. Stir in the parmesan until it melts into the sauce.

6   Serve in bowls, topped with parsley and extra parmesan.

Chicken and Chorizo with Risoni

Rice isn't typically a favourite of mine, not that I hate it but I would always prefer to eat pasta. Risoni is perfect because it makes me feel like I'm eating rice but I know it's really just small pasta. This recipe was inspired by a paella, but the price of real saffron is too crazy so we will settle for this.

SERVES 3–4
PREP TIME 10 minutes
COOK TIME 30 minutes

1 tablespoon smoked paprika
1 teaspoon ground turmeric
1 teaspoon black pepper
1 teaspoon dried oregano
1 teaspoon garlic powder
1 teaspoon salt
½ teaspoon cayenne pepper
6 skinless chicken thigh fillets
1 tablespoon olive oil
1 Spanish chorizo, diced
1 small white onion, diced
1 red capsicum, sliced into strips
2 cloves garlic, crushed
1 cup (220 g) risoni
1 tablespoon butter
2 cups (500 ml) chicken stock
sliced flat-leaf parsley, to serve

1 In a small bowl, mix the smoked paprika, turmeric, black pepper, dried oregano, garlic powder, salt and cayenne pepper. Rub this spice mix all over the chicken.

2 Heat the oil in a large frying pan over medium-high heat. Add the chicken and cook for 5–6 minutes per side, until browned and cooked through. Remove the chicken from the pan and set aside.

3 In the same pan, reduce the heat to medium. Add the chorizo and cook for 3–4 minutes, stirring occasionally, until it releases its oil and becomes slightly crispy. Add the onion, capsicum and garlic to the pan. Cook for another 5 minutes, until the vegetables soften and become fragrant.

4 Stir in the risoni, ensuring it's coated with the chorizo and vegetable mixture. Add the butter and let it melt. Pour in the chicken stock and bring the mixture to a simmer. Stir to combine, then cover the pan with a lid. Let it simmer for about 10 minutes, or until the risoni is cooked and most of the liquid is absorbed. Stir occasionally to prevent the risoni from sticking to the bottom of the pan.

5 While the risoni is cooking, slice the chicken into strips or chunks. Once the risoni is done, return the chicken to the pan and stir it into the mixture. Let everything cook together for another 2–3 minutes, until heated through.

6 Taste and adjust seasoning with salt, if needed. Serve sprinkled with parsley.

Beef Stroganoff

I remember sitting at the dinner table as a kid and chewing for what felt like hours on some beef stroganoff and being told that 'you can't leave the table until you finish your dinner'. That really turned me strogan-OFF this dish for a long time (sorry, Mum) until Pascal made it to put in the takeaway fridge at the cafe during the lockdown. The beef was tender and the sauce was tangy and creamy, and I was all over it.

SERVES 2
PREP TIME 10 minutes
COOK TIME 25 minutes

1 tablespoon olive oil
300 g steak (such as sirloin or rump), thinly sliced across the grain
1 brown onion, sliced
1 red capsicum, sliced
150 g mushrooms, sliced
2 garlic cloves, crushed
2 teaspoons paprika
200 ml beef stock
⅔ cup (160 g) sour cream
1 tablespoon dijon mustard
5 cornichons, diced
pasta, rice, mashed potato or crusty bread, to serve

1   Heat the oil in a large frying pan over medium-high heat. Add the beef to the pan in batches (don't overcrowd the pan or the temp will drop and the meat will stew) and brown it on both sides for 2–3 minutes. We want to get a really good sear as fast as possible to avoid drying out the meat. Remove from the pan and set aside.

2   In the same pan, add the onion, capsicum and mushrooms. Sauté for about 5 minutes, until the vegetables soften and the mushrooms release their moisture. Add the garlic and paprika and cook, stirring, for another minute until fragrant.

3   Pour in the stock and bring to a simmer. Let it cook for 5 minutes, allowing the sauce to reduce slightly. Stir in the sour cream and mustard. Mix well and let the sauce simmer gently for another 3–5 minutes, until creamy and thickened.

4   Add the beef back into the pan, stirring to coat in the creamy sauce. Let everything heat through for another 2–3 minutes. Season with salt and pepper to taste. Right before serving, stir in the diced cornichons for a tangy crunch.

5   Serve the beef stroganoff hot tossed through pasta, with a side of rice, mashed potatoes, or crusty bread to soak up the sauce.

For added colour and taste, you can add some extra sliced cornichons to serve.

Satay Prawn Stir-fry

RIP to my anaphylactic homies, you're really missing out on this one. Chuck this satay sauce on anything and it will be great, or use it as a dip for some fresh rice paper rolls.

SERVES 3–4
PREP TIME 15 minutes
COOK TIME 15 minutes

440 g fresh egg noodles
1 tablespoon vegetable oil
300 g raw large prawns,
    peeled and deveined
80 g baby corn, sliced lengthways
60 g snow peas, ends trimmed
1 large carrot, julienned or thinly
    sliced
½ cup (40 g) bean sprouts
¼ cup (35 g) unsalted roasted
    peanuts, lightly crushed
2–3 spring onions, sliced
lime wedges, to serve

SATAY SAUCE
½ cup (140 g) crunchy peanut butter
2 tablespoons soy sauce
2 tablespoons honey
1 tablespoon rice wine vinegar
    (or white vinegar)
1 teaspoon sesame oil
½ teaspoon garlic powder
½ teaspoon ground ginger
¼ cup (60 ml) coconut milk (or more
    for desired consistency)
1 tablespoon lime juice
pinch of chilli flakes (optional)

1. To make the satay sauce, combine the peanut butter, soy sauce, honey, vinegar, sesame oil, garlic powder and ground ginger in a medium saucepan. Place over medium heat and gently warm the mixture, stirring continuously for 2–3 minutes. Once the peanut butter has melted and the ingredients are combined, gradually add the coconut milk a tablespoon at a time, stirring to reach your desired consistency. If the sauce becomes too thick, add a splash of water. Taste and adjust seasoning with the lime juice, salt or more honey if desired. If you like it spicier, add a pinch of chilli flakes or a small splash of sriracha. Remove from heat and set aside.

2. Bring a large pot of salted water to a boil and cook the egg noodles according to package instructions (usually 3–4 minutes for fresh noodles). Reserve ¼ cup cooking water, then drain and set aside.

3. Heat the oil in a large frying pan over medium-high heat. Add the prawns and cook for 2–3 minutes on each side, until they are pink and cooked through. Remove from the pan and set aside. In the same pan, add a bit more oil if needed and toss in the baby corn, snow peas and carrot. Stir-fry for 3–4 minutes or until the vegetables are tender-crisp but still vibrant.

4. Return the prawns to the pan, followed by the cooked noodles. Add the satay sauce and toss everything together to coat in the sauce. Stir-fry for another 2–3 minutes, ensuring the sauce is evenly distributed. If it looks too dry, add a splash of the reserved cooking water to loosen it up.

5. Stir in the bean sprouts last, cooking them for just 1 minute to retain their crunch.

6. Plate the stir-fry and garnish with a generous sprinkling of crushed peanuts and sliced spring onions, with lime wedges on the side.

Creamy Beef and Broccoli Fettuccine

Fellas (or ladies), this is what you need to cook for your partner when you say 'I want to cook for you' knowing full well that they won't be impressed with your chicken and rice meal prep. Whenever my girlfriend is mad at me I'll make her this and afterwards she's still mad at me but at least she's full.

SERVES 2–3
PREP TIME 10 minutes
COOK TIME 25–30 minutes

300 g scotch fillet (about 2 cm thick), at room temperature
1 tablespoon vegetable oil
25 g unsalted butter
3 cloves garlic, crushed
2 cups (500 ml) beef stock
350 ml pure cream
200 g fettuccine
150 g baby broccolini, cut into quarters
finely grated parmesan (optional)

If the steak is not at room temperature, place it in an airtight sandwich bag and submerge it in a water bath slightly warmer than room temperature (but not hot) for 5–10 minutes to gently bring it up to temperature.

1. Generously season the steak on both sides with salt.

2. Heat a large stainless-steel pan over medium-high heat until it passes the water drop test. (Drop a small amount of water into the pan—if it beads up and glides around, the pan is hot enough. If it sizzles or evaporates too quickly, the pan is not hot enough.) Add the oil and carefully lay the steak into the pan away from yourself and sear for 2–3 minutes per side. Use a heavy object (like a protein press) to ensure even contact with the cooking surface. Remove the steak from the pan once a golden crust has formed and the internal temperature has reached at least 40°C. Set the steak aside on a plate to rest.

3. Reduce the heat to medium-low. Discard any excess oil from the pan. Add the butter to the pan and let it melt, then add the garlic and sauté for 1 minute, until fragrant. Be careful not to burn the garlic to avoid a bitter taste. Add the beef stock to the pan to deglaze, scraping up any browned bits from the bottom of the pan. Stir to combine.

4. Pour in the cream and stir well. Bring the sauce to a simmer and thicken, reducing it by a half.

5. Meanwhile, cook the fettuccine in a large pot of salted boiling water for about 2 minutes less time than the package instructions (so about 7–9 minutes) until just al dente. Reserve 1 cup pasta cooking water, then drain.

6. Add the fettucine to the thickened cream sauce, along with the baby broccolini. Stir to combine. Gradually add half the reserved pasta water, stirring constantly for 2–3 minutes, until the sauce emulsifies with the pasta water, and the pasta and broccolini are cooked through.

7. Slice the rested steak across the grain into thin strips, then cut into bite-sized pieces. Toss the steak pieces through the creamy pasta sauce just before serving. Season with salt and freshly ground black pepper to taste.

8. Serve with extra parmesan cheese sprinkled on top, if you like.

Italian
Sausage
Alfredo
Bake

Italian Sausage Alfredo Bake

Who ordered the Alfredo bake with extra sausage? Every good pasta dish
becomes a great one by adding cheese and baking it in the oven. Make sure
you grate good parmesan from a block – don't use that pre-grated stuff.

PREP TIME 15 minutes
COOK TIME 45 minutes

500 g penne
1 tablespoon olive oil
500 g Italian sausages, removed
   from casings
125 g unsalted butter
2 cloves garlic, crushed
1 cup (250 ml) thickened cream
125 g finely grated parmesan
¼ teaspoon ground nutmeg
¼ cup flat-leaf parsley, chopped
200 g fresh mozzarella, sliced or
   torn into small pieces
garlic bread and/or green salad,
   to serve

1 Preheat the oven to 180°C and grease a 33 cm × 23 cm baking dish.

2 Bring a large pot of salted water to a boil and cook the penne according
to package instructions (about 9–11 minutes) until al dente. Drain the
pasta, reserving 1 cup of pasta cooking water to use later if needed.
Set aside.

3 Meanwhile, heat the oil in a large frying pan over medium heat. Add
the sausages and cook for 6–8 minutes, breaking them up with a
wooden spoon, until browned and fully cooked. Remove from the pan
and set aside.

4 In the same pan, melt the butter over medium heat. Add the garlic and
cook for about 1 minute, until fragrant. Stir in the cream and bring to a
gentle simmer. Reduce the heat to medium-low and let it simmer for
2–3 minutes to thicken slightly. Whisk in the parmesan until melted and
smooth (leave some parmesan for step 6). Add the nutmeg and season
with salt and freshly ground black pepper to taste. If the sauce becomes
too thick, add a bit of the reserved pasta water to reach your desired
consistency.

5 In a large mixing bowl, combine the cooked penne, browned sausage
and Alfredo sauce. Stir well to coat everything evenly. Add the parsley
and toss through, saving a little for serving.

6 Transfer the pasta mixture to the prepared dish. Scatter the mozzarella
pieces evenly over the mixture, and sprinkle evenly with the extra
parmesan to create a crispy, cheesy top.

7 Bake for 20–25 minutes, or until the cheese is melted, bubbly and golden
brown on top.

8 Remove from the oven and let it rest for a few minutes. Sprinkle with the
reserved parsley before serving.

9 Serve with a side of garlic bread and/or a simple green salad with a
lemon vinaigrette.

Japanese-style Fried Chicken Bowl

I've never been to Japan but I am a huge fan of their food. The delicate balance of flavours and masterful cooking techniques inspired this extremely simplified version of a rice bowl topped with fried chicken. We both know that you'll love it.

SERVES 2
PREP TIME 15 minutes
COOK TIME 8–12 minutes

⅓ cup (80 ml) soy sauce
2 tablespoons Chinese cooking wine
2 teaspoons sesame oil
3 cloves garlic, minced
3 teaspoons ginger paste
4 chicken thigh fillets, chopped
2 tablespoons cornflour
150 ml tomato sauce
30 ml Worcestershire sauce
¼ cup (55 g) brown sugar
70 ml oyster sauce
2 cups cooked sushi rice, to serve
red cabbage, edamame, pickled
    ginger, tonkatsu sauce and
    furikake, to serve

1   In a medium bowl, combine the soy sauce, cooking wine, sesame oil, garlic and ginger. Add the chicken and toss to coat. Let the chicken marinate for at least 10 minutes, ideally 2 hours.

2   Place the cornflour into a separate small bowl (this is optional but recommended for extra crispiness). Drain off excess marinade and coat the chicken in the cornflour, pressing down gently to ensure full coverage. This will help the chicken become crispy in the air fryer.

3   Preheat the air-fryer to 220°C. Arrange the coated chicken pieces in a single layer in the air-fryer basket and spray lightly with cooking oil. Cook for 8–12 minutes, flipping halfway through and spraying the other side lightly with cooking oil, until the chicken is golden brown and crispy on both sides.

4   While the chicken is cooking, combine the tomato sauce, Worcestershire sauce, brown sugar, and oyster sauce in a small frying pan over medium heat. Stir and bring to a simmer. Cook for 5–7 minutes, until thickened. Remove from the heat.

5   While the chicken is air-frying, thinly slice the red cabbage and prepare the edamame as per package instructions.

6   Spoon the cooked sushi rice into each bowl and top with the crispy chicken. Serve with the cabbage, edamame and pickled ginger. Drizzle with tonkatsu sauce and sprinkle with furikake for added flavour and crunch.

Japanese-
style Fried
Chicken
Bowl

Cheesy Risotto

Even if you don't like risotto, it's still a very good dish to learn how to make because
without risotto you can never have arancini. Seriously though, it is another one
of those pretty basic dishes that if done right can be incredibly tasty. Use this
recipe as a base to branch out and add in your own favourite flavours.

SERVES 4
PREP TIME 10 minutes
COOK TIME 25–30 minutes

4 cups (1 litre) chicken or vegetable
    stock
1 tablespoon olive oil or butter
1 small brown onion, finely chopped
2 cloves garlic, crushed
1 cup (200 g) arborio rice
½ cup (125 ml) dry white wine
    (optional)
40 g finely grated parmesan,
    plus extra to serve
½ cup (60 g) grated cheddar cheese
chopped flat-leaf parsley, to serve
    (optional)

1   In a saucepan, heat the stock until it's hot but not boiling. Keep it on low
    heat while you make the risotto.

2   In a large saucepan, heat the olive oil or butter over medium heat. Add
    the onion and sauté for 3–4 minutes, until soft and translucent. Add the
    garlic and cook for another 30 seconds until fragrant.

3   Add the rice to the pan and stir for 1–2 minutes, allowing the rice to lightly
    toast and absorb the oil or butter.

4   If you're using wine, pour it in now, stirring constantly until it has mostly
    absorbed into the rice.

5   Start adding the hot stock, one ladleful at a time, stirring constantly. Wait
    until most of the liquid is absorbed before adding the next ladle of stock.
    Continue this process for about 18–20 minutes, or until the rice is creamy
    and al dente. You may not need all the stock, or you might need a little
    extra, so just keep checking the texture.

6   Once the rice is cooked to your liking, remove the pan from heat. Stir in
    the cheeses until they melt and the risotto becomes creamy. Taste and
    season with salt and freshly ground black pepper.

7   Serve sprinkled with the extra parmesan, and parsley if using.

Mexican Beef and Rice

If possible, I try not to leave any leftovers as I am not a huge fan of day-old food. This recipe is an exception though. Leaving time for the rice to fully soak up all of the flavours from the beef and spices is perfect for the next day. This could be your next favourite meal prep recipe.

SERVES 4
PREP TIME 10 minutes
COOK TIME about 45 minutes

200 g long-grain white rice
1 tablespoon olive oil
500 g lean beef mince (or regular
    beef mince for more richness)
1 teaspoon ground cumin
1 teaspoon smoked paprika
½ teaspoon chilli powder
    (or to taste)
1 brown onion, chopped
1 red capsicum, chopped
1–2 jalapeños, sliced (seeds removed
    for less heat, if preferred)
2 garlic cloves, crushed
400 g can diced tomatoes
500 ml beef stock (salt-reduced if
    preferred)
400 g can kidney beans or black
    beans, drained and rinsed
1 cup (120 g) grated cheddar
    (or Mexican cheese blend)
coriander leaves, lime wedges and
    sour cream, to serve

1 Wash the rice thoroughly under cold water until the water runs clear. Drain and set aside.

2 Heat the oil in a large frying pan over medium-high heat. Add the beef mince, breaking it up with a spoon as it cooks. Brown for about 5–7 minutes, until fully cooked and slightly caramelised. Tip in the cumin, smoked paprika, and chilli powder. Season with salt and freshly ground black pepper to taste. Drain off any excess fat (if necessary) and transfer the beef to a plate. Set aside.

3 Add the onion, capsicum and jalapeño to the same pan. Sauté for 3–4 minutes, until softened. Add the garlic and cook for another minute, until fragrant.

4 Add the rice to the pan and stir for 1–2 minutes to lightly toast in the spices and oil. Pour in the diced tomatoes (with juices) and the beef stock, stirring to combine. Bring it to a simmer.

5 Reduce the heat to low, cover the pan and cook for 15–20 minutes, or until the rice is tender and the liquid is absorbed. Stir occasionally to prevent sticking.

6 Stir in the beans and cooked beef. Mix well and let everything heat through for another 3–4 minutes.

7 Sprinkle the cheese over the top of the rice mixture. Cover the pan again and cook on low heat for 2–3 minutes, or until the cheese is melted and bubbly.

8 Remove the pan from heat and sprinkle with coriander. Serve with lime wedges and sour cream on the side for a burst of citrus.

One-pot Moroccan Chicken and Rice

There really isn't anything better than a one-pot meal – minimal dishes to clean up,
no running around the kitchen or dragging pots and pans out of the cupboard. This
Moroccan-inspired chicken and rice dish is perfect for an easy weeknight meal.

SERVES 4
PREP TIME 10 minutes
COOK TIME about 1 hour

1 cup (200 g) long-grain white rice
2 teaspoons ground cumin
1 teaspoon paprika
1 teaspoon ground coriander
1 teaspoon salt (or to taste)
½ teaspoon ground black pepper
½ teaspoon ground turmeric
½ teaspoon ground allspice
½ teaspoon ground ginger
½ teaspoon ground cinnamon
¼ teaspoon ground cloves
1 tablespoon honey (optional)
4 bone-in, skin-on chicken thighs
    (about 600 g)
2 tablespoons olive oil
1 onion, finely chopped
2 cloves garlic, crushed
2 cups (500 ml) chicken stock
    (or more if needed)
coriander or flat-leaf parsley,
    to serve

1   Wash the rice thoroughly under cold water until the water runs clear.
    Drain and set aside.

2   In a small bowl, mix together the cumin, paprika, coriander, salt, pepper,
    turmeric, allspice, ginger, cinnamon, cloves and optionally honey. Rub the
    spice mixture generously all over the chicken thighs.

3   In a large-heavy based pan or dutch oven, heat 1 tablespoon of the oil
    over medium-high heat. Add the chicken to the pan, skin-side down,
    and cook for 5–7 minutes, until the skin is golden brown and crispy. Flip
    the chicken and cook for another 3–4 minutes on the other side. Remove
    the chicken and set aside.

4   Heat the remaining oil in the pan. Add the onion and sauté for 5–6 minutes,
    until softened and translucent. Add the garlic and cook for 1–2 minutes,
    until fragrant.

5   Add the rice, stirring to coat in the onion, garlic and any spices left
    from the chicken. Toast the rice for 2–3 minutes, stirring occasionally, to
    enhance its flavour.

6   Pour in the chicken stock and stir well. Taste and adjust seasoning with
    additional salt or freshly ground black pepper if needed. Bring the
    mixture to a simmer.

7   Nestle the browned, seasoned chicken thighs (skin-side up) into the
    rice and stock mixture. Cover the pot with a lid and reduce the heat
    to low. Cook for 25–30 minutes, until the chicken reaches an internal
    temperature of 75°C and the rice has absorbed most of the liquid.

8   Remove from the heat and let it rest, covered, for 10 minutes to allow rice
    to finish absorbing the liquid.

9   Sprinkle with coriander or parsley for a fresh pop of colour. Serve the
    chicken thighs over the fluffy, spiced rice.

You can let the chicken marinate in the
spice mixture for 30 minutes (or even
overnight in the fridge) to allow the
spices to penetrate the meat for even
more flavour, but it's not necessary if
you're short on time.

Creamy Garlic Prawns

This is a restaurant-quality meal in under 30 minutes. Turn on the rice cooker and by the time it's cooked you'll have a perfect creamy garlic sauce and succulent prawns to pair with it – it's a real crowd-pleaser.

SERVES 2–3
PREP TIME 10 minutes
COOK TIME 15–20 minutes

250 g raw prawns, peeled and
    deveined
1 tablespoon olive oil
1 golden shallot, finely chopped
3 cloves garlic, crushed
⅓ cup (80 ml) dry white wine
200 ml pure cream
1 teaspoon chicken stock powder
20g cold butter, chopped
steamed white rice, to serve
chopped flat-leaf parsley and
    lemon wedges, to serve (optional)

1. Lightly season the prawns with salt and set aside.

2. Heat the oil in a large frying pan over medium-high heat. Add the prawns and sear for 1–2 minutes on each side, until they turn pink and opaque. Remove them from the pan and set aside.

3. Reduce the heat to medium and add a little more olive oil if necessary. Sauté the shallot until softened and translucent, about 2–3 minutes. Add the garlic and cook for another 30 seconds, until fragrant, being careful not to burn the garlic.

4. Pour in the wine, stirring to scrape up any flavourful bits left from the prawns. Let the wine simmer for 2–3 minutes, reducing by about half.

5. Stir in the cream and stock powder. Bring to a simmer then cook gently for 3–4 minutes, until thickened slightly. If the sauce gets too thick, you can add a splash of water or extra wine to loosen it up.

6. Stir in the chopped butter for extra richness, if you like. Season with salt and freshly ground black pepper to taste.

7. Return the cooked prawns to the pan, tossing them in the creamy sauce. Cook for an additional 1–2 minutes to heat through and ensure the prawns are coated in the sauce.

8. Serve the creamy garlic prawns over a bed of steamed white rice, spooning the extra sauce over the top. Sprinkle with parsley and serve with lemon wedges to squeeze over for a bit of freshness, if you like.

Honey Soy Chicken

Honey soy chicken, like the chips, is a staple in my house, the perfect balance of sweetness, spice and time spent cooking. I bet you probably already have all of the ingredients at home too.

SERVES 2
PREP TIME 10 minutes
COOK TIME 6–8 minutes

4 chicken thigh fillets, chopped
2 tablespoons soy sauce
1 tablespoon honey
1 teaspoon sesame oil
1 teaspoon ginger paste
1 teaspoon garlic powder
1 teaspoon onion powder
1 teaspoon chilli powder
½ teaspoon MSG (optional)
½ teaspoon ground white pepper
1 tablespoon cornflour
1 tablespoon vegetable or canola oil
steamed white rice and sesame
 seeds, to serve

1 In a medium bowl, combine the chicken with the soy sauce, honey, sesame oil, ginger paste, garlic powder, onion powder, chilli powder, MSG (if using), white pepper and cornflour. Mix well to coat the chicken thoroughly with the marinade. Allow the chicken to marinate for 5–10 minutes, to absorb the flavours.

2 While the chicken is marinating, place a large frying pan over high heat and let it heat up for about 5 minutes. Once hot, add the oil and swirl it around to coat the bottom of the pan.

3 Add the chicken to the pan in a single layer allowing to cook, undisturbed for 1-2 minutes. Continue to cook for another 5-6 minutes, stirring occasionally, until it is cooked through and golden brown. The marinade should begin to caramelise and turn a darker brown colour, coating the chicken with a sticky glaze.

4 Serve the chicken over steamed white rice, sprinkled with sesame seeds for a finishing touch.

Korean Beef Bowl in under 25 Minutes

As the self-proclaimed laziest person in the world, meals like this are a fantasy.
You can decide to cook this and be eating it 25 minutes later! Sounds like a
win to me. The beef mince is so packed with flavour and the vegetables add
a nice fresh crunch. Cook the rice yourself, or use microwave rice.

SERVES 2
PREP TIME 10 minutes
COOK TIME 15 minutes

2 tablespoons sesame oil
3 cloves garlic, crushed
2 tablespoons finely grated ginger
500 g lean beef mince
¼ cup (60 ml) soy sauce
2 tablespoons brown sugar or honey
1 tablespoon rice wine vinegar
1 tablespoon gochujang (Korean
   fermented chilli paste), or to taste
2 cups cooked rice
1 tablespoon sesame seeds
2 spring onions, finely sliced
1 small cucumber, thinly sliced
1 small carrot, julienned
¼ cup (60g) kimchi (optional)
1 soft-boiled egg, halved (optional)

1. Heat the sesame oil in a large frying pan or wok over medium-high heat. Add the garlic and ginger, and sauté for 1–2 minutes, until fragrant. Add the beef mince to the pan. Stir-fry for 5–7 minutes, using a wooden spoon to break it up as it cooks, until browned and cooked through.

2. While the beef is cooking, combine the soy sauce, brown sugar (or honey), vinegar and gochujang in a small bowl. Stir until the sugar dissolves and the ingredients are well combined.

3. Pour the sauce over the mince and stir well to combine. Let it simmer for an additional 2–3 minutes, allowing the sauce to thicken slightly and coat the beef.

4. Divide the cooked rice between bowls. Top each bowl with the beef mixture, making sure to spread it evenly over the rice.

5. Top with sesame seeds, spring onions, cucumber and carrot. For an extra touch, add a small spoonful of kimchi on the side and half a boiled egg for added richness.

Spicy Beef and Beans

Beans, beans, they're good for your heart. The more you eat, the more you start
to . . . think 'wow, these would be really good with beef and chorizo'. Spicy beans are
what I like to think of as the perfect meal, full of protein and fibre, spicy (but not
too spicy) and you can eat them with anything. My favourite way to serve these
is with a side, or whole loaf, of toasted sourdough bread with lots of butter.

SERVES 4
PREP TIME 15 minutes
COOK TIME 45 minutes

2 chorizo sausages, chopped
300 g scotch fillet, cut into roughly
   3-cm pieces
1 brown onion, finely diced
4 garlic cloves, grated
1 tablespoon ground coriander
1 tablespoon ground cumin
1 tablespoon paprika
1 tablespoon dried oregano
1 tablespoon chipotle in adobo
   sauce, finely chopped
700 g bottle passata
4 cups (1 litre) beef stock
1 bunch coriander, washed,
   stems and leaves separated
400 g can kidney beans,
   drained and rinsed
steamed rice or toasted sourdough,
   to serve
Greek-style feta or sour cream,
   to serve (optional)

1 Heat a large heavy-based pan or dutch oven over medium heat. Add the chorizo and cook, stirring occasionally, for about 5 minutes, until the chorizo releases its oils and begins to crisp up. Remove the chorizo from the pan and set it aside, leaving the rendered fat in the pot.

2 Add the scotch fillet and season well with salt and freshly ground black pepper. Sear in the chorizo fat for 3–4 minutes on all sides until browned. Remove from the pan and set it aside with the chorizo.

3 Add the onion to the pan and cook for about 5 minutes, until softened and translucent. Add the garlic and cook for another 1–2 minutes, until fragrant.

4 Stir in the ground coriander, cumin, paprika, oregano and chipotle in adobo sauce. Cook for 1 minute, stirring frequently, to toast the spices and enhance their flavours.

5 Pour in the passata and beef stock, stirring to combine. Bring the mixture to a simmer, scraping up any brown bits from the bottom of the pan (this is your one-way ticket to flavour town).

6 Chop the coriander stems and add to the pan with the chorizo and beef. Stir everything together, cover, and simmer on low heat, uncovered for 10–15 minutes, or until the sauce slightly thickens.

7 Add the beans to the pan and stir gently to combine. Cook, uncovered, for a further 10 minutes, to heat the beans through and allow the flavours to get to know each other.

8 Taste and adjust seasoning with salt and freshly ground black pepper as needed. If you prefer a thicker sauce, allow it to simmer uncovered for a bit longer.

9 Serve the spicy beef and beans over rice for a complete meal, or alongside toasted sourdough to soak up the delicious sauce. Sprinkle with the coriander leaves, and crumbled Greek-style feta or a dollop of sour cream for a creamy, cooling contrast.

Crispy Chicken Thighs in Lemon Herb Pan Sauce

A pan sauce feels like a hidden treasure. Most of the time all of the crispy browned bits on the bottom of the pan get scrubbed away with soap and a scrub daddy. This recipe shows you how to maximise the flavour in a one pan dish by turning those forgotten brown bits into a delicious lemon herb pan sauce.

SERVES 4
PREP TIME 10 minutes
COOK TIME 30 minutes

4 bone-in, skin-on chicken thighs
2 tablespoons olive oil
2 golden shallots, finely chopped
2 cloves garlic, crushed
½ cup (120 ml) dry white wine
2 cups (500 ml) chicken stock
4 tablespoons unsalted butter
4 tablespoons lemon juice
1 cup flat-leaf parsley, finely
   chopped
lemon wedges, to serve (optional)

1 Pat the chicken thighs dry with paper towels. This helps to achieve a crispy skin. Season both sides generously with salt and freshly ground black pepper.

2 Heat the oil in a large frying pan over medium-high heat. Carefully place the chicken thighs, skin-side down, in the pan. Sear for 5–7 minutes, or until the skin is golden and crispy. Flip the chicken and cook for 5–7 minutes on the other side, until the chicken is mostly cooked through. Remove the chicken from the pan and set aside. Discard any excess fat in the pan, leaving a thin layer to make the sauce.

3 Reduce the heat to medium. Add the shallot and cook, stirring, for about 2 minutes, until softened and translucent. Add the garlic and cook for 30 seconds, until fragrant. Pour in the white wine, scraping the bottom of the pan to release any crispy bits (this is called the fond). Simmer for about 2 minutes, to reduce slightly. Add the chicken stock and bring to a simmer. Cook for about 5 minutes, until reduced by about half.

4 Add the butter and stir to incorporate, creating a rich, velvety sauce. Stir in the lemon juice and parsley, and season with salt and pepper to taste.

5 Place the chicken thighs back into the pan, skin-side up. Spoon some sauce over the chicken, then cover the pan and let it simmer on low heat for 5–7 minutes, or until the chicken reaches an internal temperature of 75°C and is fully cooked through.

6 Serve the chicken thighs with a generous spoonful of the lemon herb sauce. Garnish with additional parsley and a wedge of lemon if desired. Pair with roasted vegetables, mashed potatoes, or rice for a complete meal.

Portuguese Chicken and Fries

Think of this as exactly what Nando's wishes it was: vibrant spicy chicken with crispy skin served with crunchy fries and a spicy dipping sauce. Piri piri chillies aren't widely available in Australia, unless you grow them yourself, but bird's-eye chillies are easy to find and they do the trick.

SERVES 3–4
PREP TIME 15 minutes plus 1 hour
  marinating
COOK TIME 45 minutes

PIRI PIRI CHICKEN
5–6 bird's-eye chillies
  (or fresh piri piri), stems removed
3 cloves garlic, crushed
½ small onion, roughly diced
2 dried bay leaves, crushed
juice of 1 lemon
2 teaspoons olive oil
1 tablespoon smoked paprika
1 teaspoon dried oregano
1 teaspoon salt
1 teaspoon fresh cracked black pepper
3–4 chicken maryland supreme
  (skin on, about 350 g each)

TWICE FRIED FRIES
5–6 brushed potatoes, washed and
  peeled
3 teaspoons salt (or to taste)
vegetable oil, for frying

DIPPING SAUCE
1–2 tablespoons reserved piri piri
  marinade (from step 1)
¾–1 cup (225 g–300 g) mayonnaise
  (adjust depending on desired
  spiciness)

Serve the piri piri chicken with a generous portion of the fries and a side of the creamy dipping sauce. You can also add a fresh side salad or some steamed vegetables to balance the heat and richness of the meal.

1 For the piri piri chicken, combine the chillies, garlic, onion and bay leaves in a blender or food processor. Blend until smooth but still slightly chunky. Add the lemon juice, oil, paprika, oregano, salt and pepper. Blend until smooth and well combined. Reserve 1–2 tablespoons of the chilli marinade for the dipping sauce.

2 Pat the chicken dry with paper towels. Use the remaining chilli marinade to thoroughly coat the chicken, ensuring the sauce is rubbed all over and under the skin where possible. I would advise wearing gloves for this step because it can get pretty messy. Marinate the chicken in the fridge for at least 1 hour, or ideally overnight for the best flavour.

3 To make the fries, cut the potatoes into 5 mm thick strips (like shoestring fries). Soak them in a large bowl of cold water for at least 30 minutes, but ideally for 1 hour. This helps remove excess starch and ensures fluffier, crispier fries.

4 Preheat the oven to 220°C. Place the chicken skin side up on a rimmed baking tray lined with baking paper. Roast for 40–45 minutes, basting with the liquid in the tray every 15 minutes. The chicken is ready when the skin is golden brown and crispy, and the internal temperature reaches 75°C. Set chicken aside to rest for 5–10 minutes.

5 Meanwhile, heat the oil in a deep-fryer or a large pot to 160°C. Drain the soaked fries and pat them completely dry with paper towels to avoid splattering. Cook the fries in batches for 4–5 minutes, or until they are cooked through but not yet crispy or golden. They should be soft but not browned. Use a large slotted spoon to remove the fries from the oil, and drain them on a baking tray lined with paper towel. Let them cool for about 10 minutes.

6 Heat the oil to 190°C for the second fry. Cook the fries again in batches for 2–3 minutes, or until golden brown and crispy. Drain on a clean paper towel-lined tray. While the fries are still hot, season them with 3 teaspoons salt, or to taste.

7 For the dipping sauce, in a small bowl, combine the reserved chilli marinade with the mayonnaise. Adjust the amount of mayonnaise depending on how spicy you want the sauce. Stir until well combined. Taste and adjust seasoning, adding more marinade if desired for extra heat.

Loaded Cheeseburger Fries

I eat this way more than I would like to admit. It hits that burger craving whilst still being a more balanced meal with far fewer calories than takeaway. This recipe also went nuts online, getting over 14 million views on my social media, so it felt like a must-add to this book.

SERVES 2
PREP TIME 30 minutes
COOK TIME 15 minutes

½ cup shredded iceberg lettuce
finely diced white onion, to taste
finely diced pickles, to taste
2 teaspoons sesame seeds

FRIES
4 potatoes, peeled
2 teaspoons garlic powder
1 tablespoon paprika
2 teaspoons salt
1 teaspoon white pepper
2 tablespoons olive oil

SAUCE
½ cup (150 g) mayonnaise
2 tablespoons diced pickles
2 tablespoons diced white onion
½ teaspoon dijon mustard
½ teaspoon paprika
2 teaspoons garlic powder
2 teaspoons pickle juice

BEEF
1 teaspoon olive oil
360 g beef mince
2 teaspoons paprika
1 teaspoon garlic powder
1 teaspoon celery salt
½ teaspoon white pepper
100 g mozzarella, shredded

1   To make the fries, preheat the air-fryer to 200°C. Cut the potatoes into 5 mm thick strips (like shoestring fries). Place into a large bowl and sprinkle with garlic powder, paprika, salt and pepper. Drizzle with the oil and toss to coat evenly. Place the fries in the air-fryer basket and cook for 15 minutes, shaking the basket occasionally so they cook evenly, or until golden and crisp . After cooking, remove the fries and season with a pinch of salt.

2   To make the sauce, place all the ingredients into a bowl and stir until evenly combined. Set aside.

3   For the beef, heat the oil in a non-stick frying pan over high heat. Add the beef mince and season with a pinch of salt. Cook, breaking it up with a spatula, until browned and crispy. Add the paprika, garlic powder, celery salt and pepper. Stir to combine. Sprinkle the mozzarella over the beef and cook for 1–2 minutes, until the cheese is melted and bubbly.

4   In each serving bowl, layer the crispy fries and top with the cheesy beef mixture. Add a generous amount of the sauce on top. Sprinkle with the lettuce, onion and pickles. Finish by sprinkling sesame seeds over the top for extra crunch.

Squeeze as much tomato sauce as you like to serve.

Stuffed Chicken Caprese Tray Bake

If you love to get baked, TRAY baked, then this is the meal for you. I love simple cooking and this recipe is the epitome of it. Perfect rolls of chicken breast stuffed with cherry tomatoes, pesto and cheese all wrapped in crispy prosciutto.

SERVES 4
PREP TIME 15 minutes
COOK TIME 20–25 minutes

4 chicken breast fillets
¼ cup (65 g) basil pesto (page 202)
200 g fresh mozzarella, sliced
200 g cherry tomatoes, halved
8 slices prosciutto
olive oil, for drizzling

1   Preheat the oven to 200°C. Butterfly the chicken breasts by slicing them horizontally, without going all the way through, down one long side. Open them out and pound flat to an even thickness using a meat mallet or rolling pin. Season both sides with salt and freshly ground black pepper.

2   Spread a thin layer of basil pesto over the inside of each chicken breast. Place a few slices of mozzarella on top of the pesto, then scatter the halved cherry tomatoes over the mozzarella. Season the tomatoes lightly with a pinch of salt.

3   Roll the chicken breasts up tightly, securing the filling inside. Wrap each rolled chicken breast with 2 slices of prosciutto to hold everything together. Use toothpicks or bamboo skewers to pin the prosciutto in place. It will shrink around the chicken during cooking and the skewers can be removed before serving.

4   Place the chicken onto a baking tray lined with baking paper. Drizzle with a little olive oil. Bake for 20–25 minutes, or until the internal temperature of the chicken reaches 75°C and the prosciutto is crispy.

SERVING SUGGESTIONS:

ROASTED VEGETABLES

Serve the stuffed chicken with a side of roasted vegetables like chopped zucchini, sliced capsicum and/or asparagus. Simply toss them with olive oil, season with salt and pepper and roast in the same oven for 20–25 minutes.

SIDE SALAD

Pair with a fresh, light salad of mixed greens, rocket and a simple balsamic vinaigrette (see page 207) to balance the richness of the chicken.

GARLIC BREAD OR CRISPY POTATOES

For a heartier meal, serve alongside garlic bread or crispy roasted potatoes. The potatoes can be tossed with olive oil, rosemary, and garlic, then roasted until golden and crispy. Give them a 30-minute head start in the oven.

Chipotle
Roasted
Chicken Thigh
Tray Bake

Chipotle Roasted Chicken Thigh Tray Bake with Spicy Citrus Rice

Back when I was working in a cafe we would have a 'chipotle mayo' which was really just smoked paprika and mayonnaise. It worked because it was the same colour and no one knew the difference. I now know what chipotle chillies actually taste like and I feel bad for everyone who ate that sauce. This tray bake has REAL chipotle chillies and is full of REAL flavour.

SERVES 4
PREP TIME 20 minutes plus 15 mins–2 hours marinating
COOK TIME 40 minutes

1 red capsicum, seeded and
   cut into chunks
1 yellow capsicum, seeded and
   cut into chunks
1 green capsicum, seeded and
   cut into chunks
1 large brown onion, quartered
olive oil, for drizzling
200 g cherry tomatoes

CHIPOTLE ROASTED CHICKEN THIGHS
6–8 bone-in, skin-on chicken thighs
2 tablespoons olive oil
2–3 chipotle chillies in adobo sauce,
   finely chopped (adjust for heat
   preference)
1 tablespoon honey
1 tablespoon soy sauce
2 teaspoons ground cumin
2 teaspoons smoked paprika
1 teaspoon garlic powder
1 teaspoon onion powder

SPICY CITRUS RICE
1 cup (200 g) basmati rice
1 tablespoon olive oil
1 small red chilli, finely chopped
   (optional)
finely grated zest and juice of
   1 orange
finely grated zest and juice of 1 lime
2 cups (500 ml) chicken stock

1 Preheat the oven to 220°C.

2 To make the chipotle chicken, pat the chicken thighs dry with paper towel. Season both sides generously with salt and pepper.

3 In a small bowl, mix together the olive oil, chilli in adobo sauce, honey, soy sauce, cumin, paprika, garlic powder and onion powder. Stir until well combined.

4 Wearing gloves, rub the chipotle marinade all over the chicken thighs, ensuring they are thoroughly coated. Let the chicken marinate for at least 15 minutes, or up to 2 hours in the fridge for deeper flavour.

5 Toss the capsicums and onion with olive oil, and season with salt and pepper. Arrange them on a large roasting tray.

6 Place the marinated chicken thighs on top of the vegetables, skin-side up. Add the whole cherry tomatoes to the tray around the chicken and vegetables.

7 Roast for 30–35 minutes or until the chicken thighs reach an internal temperature of 75°C and the skin is starting to brown. Make sure the vegetables are tender and lightly caramelised.

8 Turn the oven to the grill setting on high and cook for an additional 5 minutes to crisp up the skin. Keep an eye on the chicken to ensure it doesn't burn.

9   Meanwhile, for the spicy citrus rice, rinse the rice under cold water until the water runs clear. Drain well. In a medium saucepan, heat the olive oil over medium heat. Add the chilli (if using) and sauté for 1 minute, until fragrant. Add the rice to the pan and toast for 1–2 minutes, stirring occasionally.

10 Stir in the orange zest and juice, lime zest and juice and the chicken stock. Bring to the boil, then reduce the heat to low. Cover and cook for 12–15 minutes, or until the rice is tender and the liquid is absorbed. Uncover and fluff the grains of rice with a fork.

11 Plate the crispy chicken thighs with the roasted capsicum, onion and tomatoes. Serve alongside a generous helping of spicy citrus rice.

Balance the bold, smoky flavours and spice of the dish by serving it with a cooling dollop of sour cream or Greek yoghurt, and add a side of black bean and corn salsa (page 26) for a fresh, zesty contrast that complements the citrusy rice and chipotle chicken perfectly.

Arancini

Arancini has to be the ultimate leftovers hack for two reasons: it's deep-fried and is full of gooey cheese. This is a fool-proof format to turn any leftover risotto into golden fried balls that will have you wishing you made a bigger pot of risotto.

SERVES 4 (makes about 12–15)
PREP TIME 20 minutes
COOK TIME 10–15 minutes

2 cups cold leftover risotto
20 g finely grated parmesan
   (optional, for extra flavour)
75 g mozzarella, cut into small cubes
   (roughly 5g each)
½ cup (75 g) plain flour
2 eggs, lightly beaten
1 cup (75 g) panko breadcrumbs
vegetable oil, to fry
chopped parsley (optional)
warm tomato pasta sauce (or your
   favourite dipping sauce), to serve

1. Take a small portion of the risotto mixture (about a tablespoon) and flatten it slightly in your hand. Place a small cube of mozzarella in the centre, then mould the risotto around it to form a ball. The ball should be about the size of a golf ball or slightly smaller. Repeat until all the risotto is used.

2. Set up a crumbing station with three shallow dishes – one with the flour, one with the beaten eggs and one with breadcrumbs (add parmesan if you like).

3. Roll each rice ball in the flour first, then dip it into the beaten egg, and finally coat it thoroughly with the breadcrumbs. This will create a crispy outer layer when fried.

4. Heat about 5–7 cm of oil in a deep saucepan or deep-fryer over medium heat. To test if the oil is hot enough, drop a small piece of bread into the oil – if it browns in about 30 seconds, the oil is ready.

5. Fry the arancini in batches, making sure not to overcrowd the pan. Fry them for 3–4 minutes, turning occasionally, until golden brown and crispy on all sides. Use a large slotted spoon to remove the arancini from the oil and drain them on paper towel.

6. Once all the arancini are fried, serve them hot with sauce for dipping. Sprinkle with parsley if desired.

If you are making these from leftover risotto, it will be chilled and firm. If you are making risotto especially for this, chill it for at least 30 minutes, so it won't be too soft to handle.

Pasta Bake (Poor Man's Lasagne)

Did you cook way too much pasta last night and now there's 'leftovers'? Let's turn that Tupperware full of cold spaghetti into something that would make someone's Italian grandparents furious. Choose one of the base sauces, mix it with the pasta, and top with a cheesy mornay sauce. Too easy!

SERVES 4–6
PREP TIME 20 minutes
COOK TIME 30-35 minutes

TOMATO SAUCE (base option 1)
1 tablespoon olive oil
1 small onion, finely chopped
2 cloves garlic, crushed
400 g can crushed tomatoes
   (or passata)
1 teaspoon dried oregano or basil
   (or fresh, finely chopped)
40 g finely grated parmesan
   (optional)

CREAM SAUCE (base option 2)
1 tablespoon olive oil
1 small onion, finely chopped
2 cloves garlic, crushed
1 cup (250 ml) thickened cream
   (full cream or light)
40 g finely grated parmesan
1 teaspoon dried thyme or rosemary

PESTO SAUCE (base option 3)
½ cup (130 g) pesto (store-bought or
   homemade)
½ cup (125 ml) thickened cream
40 g finely grated parmesan

MORNAY SAUCE (for top layer)
50 g butter
⅓ cup (50 g) plain flour
2 cups (500 ml) milk (full cream
   is best)
1 cup (120 g) grated cheese
   (cheddar, mozzarella or a mixture)
¼ teaspoon ground nutmeg
   (optional)

PASTA BAKE
500 g leftover cooked pasta
   (or 250 g pasta, cooked)
1 cup (120 g) grated cheese
   (mozzarella or cheddar)

1. Preheat the oven to 180°C. Grease a 30 cm × 20 cm baking dish with butter or oil.

2. Prepare the chosen base sauce, as below, and set aside:

TOMATO SAUCE Heat the olive oil in a saucepan over medium heat. Add the onion and garlic. Sauté for about 5 minutes, until soft and fragrant. Add the tomatoes (or passata) and herbs. Reduce heat and simmer for 5–10 minutes, until thickened. Stir in parmesan, if using. Season with salt and freshly ground black pepper to taste.

CREAM SAUCE Heat the olive oil in a saucepan over medium heat. Add the onion and garlic. Sauté for about 5 minutes, until soft and fragrant. Add the cream and bring to a simmer. Stir in the parmesan and herbs. Simmer gently for a few minutes to thicken slightly. Season with salt and freshly ground black pepper to taste.

PESTO SAUCE In a bowl, mix the pesto with cream and parmesan. Season with salt and freshly ground black pepper to taste.

3. To make the mornay sauce, melt the butter in a saucepan over medium heat. Add the flour and whisk until smooth (this is called a roux). Cook for 1–2 minutes, stirring constantly, to cook out the raw flour taste. Gradually pour in the milk, whisking continuously to avoid lumps. Bring to a simmer and cook for 5 minutes, stirring often, until thickened. Remove from the heat and stir in the cheese until melted. Add the nutmeg (if using) and season with salt and freshly ground black pepper to taste.

4. To assemble the pasta bake, spread a thin layer of base sauce on the bottom of the baking dish. Toss the pasta with the base sauce and spread half of it into the dish. Sprinkle with half the cheese. Spread remaining pasta over in an even layer. Pour the mornay sauce over the pasta, covering it completely. Sprinkle with the remaining cheese.

5. Bake for 20–25 minutes, until the top is golden brown and bubbling. If you want a crisper top, you can grill it for a couple of minutes at the end of cooking.

6. Stand the pasta bake for 5 minutes to cool slightly, before serving.

Elevated Basics

A Very
Sacrilegious
Lasagne

A Very Sacrilegious Lasagne

In my family, when it's your birthday you get to choose what's for dinner. Every year I would ask Mum to make lasagne and by the eighth time I didn't get asked anymore, I just got lasagne. My love for lasagne only grew when the whole family went to an Italian restaurant in Mittagong called Esco Pazzo. I haven't had lasagne that good in years but through many, many attempts I think I have created the best recipe possible (you be the judge).

SERVES 6–8
PREP TIME 45 minutes
COOK TIME 1 hour 45 minutes–3 hours 45 minutes

MEAT SAUCE
500 g pork mince
500 g beef mince
1 brown onion, finely diced
2 stalks celery, finely diced
1 carrot, finely diced
4 cloves garlic, crushed
2 cups (500 ml) beef stock
2 × 700 g bottles passata
1 bunch basil, leaves picked
1 bunch thyme, leaves picked
½ bunch oregano, leaves picked
1 tablespoon dried rosemary
2 teaspoons dried chilli flakes

BÉCHAMEL SAUCE
100 g unsalted butter
100 g plain flour
4 cups (1 litre) milk
½ teaspoon ground nutmeg
½ teaspoon white pepper

TO ASSEMBLE
375 g packet (8) fresh lasagne sheets
500 g mozzarella, grated

1 To make the meat sauce, heat a large heavy-based pan over medium-high heat. Add the meat and cook until all the moisture has evaporated and meat is a deep brown colour. Transfer to a large bowl and set aside.

2 Reduce the heat to low and add the onion, celery and carrot with a pinch of salt. Sweat for 5–10 mins until the onion is translucent and carrot is soft enough to squeeze to mush.

3 Add in garlic and cook for 1 minute. Return the meat to the pan and stir to combine.

4 Add the beef stock, passata and about half the volume in water to rinse out the inside of the bottles. Stir in the herbs and chilli flakes.

5 Bring to a simmer and place a lid on, but tilt it so the pan is about 90 per cent covered. Cook for at least 1 hour but ideally up to 3 hours, stirring occasionally. Season with salt and pepper to taste.

6 Preheat the oven to 180°C. Lightly grease a 30 cm × 22 cm (5 cm deep) baking dish with oil.

7 For the béchamel sauce, melt the butter in a large saucepan over medium heat until foamy (almost boiling). Add the flour and whisk to combine. Cook for 1–2 minutes, stirring constantly, to cook out the raw flour taste.

8 Add the milk in 3 stages, the first addition being the least milk (roughly ½–1 cup) and the final stage being the most (2 cups). Stir well to combine and make sure there are no lumps before adding more milk.

9 Bring to the boil and cook for 1 minute. Take off the heat and stir in the nutmeg and white pepper. Season with salt to taste.

10 To assemble, cover the base of the dish with a thin layer of meat sauce then a layer of lasagne sheets, trimming to fit as needed. Add a layer of béchamel, meat sauce and mozzarella, reserving roughly ¼ for the top layer. Repeat 3 times, leaving off the final layer of mozzarella for now.

11 Cover with foil and bake for 30 minutes. Uncover, top with the remaining mozzarella and bake for another 10 minutes, to melt and crisp up the cheese.

Time your béchamel sauce to be ready just before assembling the lasagne. If it sits too long, it can thicken too much or develop a skin, making it hard to spread evenly.

Duck Ragout

If we are talking date night meals, we are talking duck ragout. If you make this for someone,
they are guaranteed to fall in love with you, trust me. You can substitute the duck for beef
or lamb but there's something about the texture and flavour of duck that can't be beaten.

SERVES 4
PREP TIME 20 minutes
COOK TIME 2½–3½ hours

4 duck marylands (joined thigh
   and drumstick)
1 tablespoon duck fat (or any oil)
1 brown onion, diced
1 carrot, diced
2 sticks celery, diced
6 cloves garlic, crushed
2 tablespoons tomato paste
1 cup (250 ml) red wine
1 tablespoon balsamic vinegar
4 cups (1 litre) chicken stock
½ bunch thyme, leaves chopped
   (or 1 tablespoon dried)
1 tablespoon oregano leaves
20–40 g finely grated parmesan

PANGRATTATO
50 g butter
1 cup (75 g) panko breadcrumbs
1 teaspoon salt
¼ cup basil and thyme leaves
   (combined), chopped

This is delicious served over
pappardelle. Cook in a pot of water
until just al dente, then add to the
ragout to finish cooking.

1. Season the duck well with salt and freshly ground black pepper on both
   sides. Heat the duck fat in a large deep frying pan over medium heat and
   sear duck until golden brown. Set aside on a plate.

2. Add the onion, carrot and celery to the pan and season lightly with a
   pinch of salt to draw out the moisture. Reduce the heat to low and gently
   sweat for 5–10 minutes until soft and slightly caramelised. Add the garlic
   and cook for 30 seconds, until fragrant.

3. Push everything to the edges to create a space in the middle. Add the
   tomato paste and cook, stirring, for about 1 minute until lightly toasted.
   Combine with the vegetables.

4. Deglaze with the red wine, making sure to scrape all the bits off the
   bottom. Bring to a simmer and cook for about 3 minutes, until reduced by
   half.

5. Add the vinegar, stock and herbs. Stir to combine then arrange duck
   skin side up in the pan. Bring to a simmer then cover with a cartouche
   (a round of baking paper with a hole in the middle, to reduce
   evaporation) and a lid. Simmer for 2–3 hours over low heat, until the
   meat begins to fall off the bone.

6. Remove the duck from the pan and let it cool slightly (if you're a coward).
   Pull the meat from the bones, lightly shredding it.

7. Transfer the sauce to a blender and blend until smooth. Return to the pan
   with the shredded duck meat and parmesan, stirring to combine.

8. For the pangrattato, melt the butter in a frying pan over medium heat.
   Add the breadcrumbs and stir so they absorb the butter. Add the salt
   and herbs, stirring to combine. Gently toast the breadcrumbs, stirring
   frequently, until golden brown. Remove from the heat and set aside.

9. Serve ragout sprinkled with the pangrattato.

Osso Buco

This is a recipe to test your patience. It's a little tricky and quite time consuming
but the result will blow you away. One of the most difficult parts is getting the veal
shanks out of the sauce without them falling apart because they will be insanely soft!
This is great served over creamy mashed potato, saffron risotto, polenta or pasta.

SERVES 4
PREP TIME 20 minutes
COOK TIME 1½–2½ hours

4 veal shanks (osso buco)
¼ cup (35 g) plain flour
1 tablespoon olive oil
1 brown onion, diced
1 carrot, diced
2 sticks celery, diced
3 cloves garlic, crushed
1 tablespoon tomato paste
1 cup (250 ml) dry white wine
   (I used sav blanc)
1 210 g can crushed tomato
300 ml chicken bone broth or good
   quality stock
½ bunch thyme, leaves chopped

GREMOLATA
½ cup finely chopped parsley
2 cloves garlic, finely chopped
1 teaspoon finely grated lemon zest
3–4 tablespoons olive oil, to taste
½ teaspoon salt

1 Preheat the oven to 180°C. Tie the veal shanks tightly with kitchen string to keep them a neat round shape and hold them together during cooking. Season with salt and freshly ground black pepper on both sides then lightly coat in flour, shaking off the excess.

2 Heat the oil in a large heavy-based ovenproof pan (like a dutch oven) over medium-high heat. Sear the veal on each side until a good brown crust forms. Remove from the pan and set aside.

3 Reduce the heat to medium. Add the onion, carrot and celery to the pan and sauté for a few minutes, until soft. Add the garlic and cook for 30 seconds. Create a space in the middle of the veggies and add the tomato paste. Cook, stirring, for 30 seconds then stir it into the other ingredients.

4 Deglaze the pan with the white wine, scraping all the brown bits (fond) off the bottom of the pan. Add the tomato, broth and thyme. Return the meat to the pan, leaving the tops exposed.

5 Bring to a simmer then cover with a cartouche (a round of baking paper with a hole in the middle, to reduce evaporation) and a lid. Transfer to the oven and bake for 1½ hours, until the meat is very tender.

6 Transfer the meat to a plate, cover with foil and keep warm. Cook the sauce over medium heat, uncovered, for 10–15 minutes, until thickened and reduced slightly. Season with salt and freshly ground black pepper to taste.

7 To make the gremolata, combine the ingredients in a small bowl. Serve spooned over the osso buco.

Chilli Con Carne

I could (and have) just eaten a whole bowl of this for dinner. No rice, no bread, just chilli. There have been many iterations of this recipe over the years, but I finally landed on one that's worthy of writing down. Throw away your mum's chilli recipe, because this is the only one you'll ever need.

SERVES 4–6
PREP TIME 20 minutes
COOK TIME 1 hour 15 minutes–
  2 hours 15 minutes

2 tablespoons olive oil
500 g beef mince
1 brown onion, diced
1 red capsicum, diced
1 green capsicum, diced
1 poblano chilli, diced (or swap for
  a yellow capsicum)
4 cloves garlic
2 tablespoons paprika
2 tablespoons ground cumin
1 teaspoon chipotle chilli powder
1 teaspoon ground black pepper
½ teaspoon ground ginger
1 teaspoon chopped chipotle in
  adobo sauce
400 g can diced tomatoes
2 cups (500 ml) beef stock
½ bunch coriander, washed, stems
  and leaves separated
1 teaspoon cocoa powder (trust me)
400 g can kidney beans, semi-
  drained
steamed white rice and sour cream,
  to serve
1 lime, cut into wedges

1 Heat the oil in a large heavy-based pan over medium heat. Add the mince and cook, breaking up any lumps with a wooden spoon, until well browned. Transfer to a bowl.

2 Add the onion to the pan and sweat for about 3 minutes, scraping the bottom to release the brown bits, until translucent.

3 Add capsicum and poblano chilli, and cook for 3–5 minutes, until softened. Stir in the garlic and cook for 1 minute (avoid burning the garlic).

4 Stir in the spices and chipotle in adobo, toasting for 30 seconds to 1 minute. Keep it moving around to avoid the spices burning. Return the beef and mix to combine, then pour in the tomato and stock.

5 Chop the coriander stems and add to the pan with the cocoa powder. (I know it sounds weird, but the bitterness of the cocoa will neutralise the acidity from the tomatoes and help balance the flavours in the dish.)

6 Bring to the boil then reduce heat to low. Simmer while covered for 1 hour (but ideally 2 hours), stirring occasionally.

7 Add the kidney beans (and bit of the canning liquid) in the last 20 minutes of cooking. Season with salt to taste.

8 Serve with steamed white rice, sour cream, coriander leaves and lime wedges.

Cottage Pie

It's not a shepherd's pie – those are made with lamb mince (shepherds herd sheep).
This is the only thing I want to be coming home to on a cold winter's day. Crispy,
crumbly topping, creamy mash and a flavourful mince is the perfect winter warmer.

SERVES 6–8
PREP TIME 20 minutes
COOK TIME 1½–2½ hours

FILLING
2 tablespoons olive oil
1 kg beef mince
1 large brown onion, diced
2 carrots, diced
2 sticks celery, finely diced
3 cloves garlic, minced
1 bunch fresh thyme, leaves finely
    chopped (or 1 tablespoon dried
    thyme)
2 tablespoons (30 ml) Worcestershire
    sauce
½ cup (140 g) tomato paste
3 dried bay leaves
1 cup (120 g) frozen peas

MASHED POTATO TOPPING
1 kg brushed potatoes, peeled and
    cut into even-sized cubes
100 g cold unsalted butter (or more
    to taste), chopped
100 ml warm milk (for loosening the
    mash if needed)

CRUMB TOPPING
½ cup (35 g) panko breadcrumbs
20 g finely grated parmesan
1 tablespoon fresh or dried thyme

1 To make the filling, heat the oil in a large heavy-based ovenproof pan (like a dutch oven) over medium-high heat. Add the beef mince and cook, breaking up any lumps with a wooden spoon, until well browned.

2 Add the onion, carrot, celery and garlic. Cook for about 5 minutes, stirring occasionally, until the vegetables begin to soften.

3 Stir in the thyme, Worcestershire sauce, tomato paste and bay leaves. Cook for 1–2 minutes, allowing the tomato paste to deepen in colour.

4 Pour in enough water to just cover the meat mixture. Stir to combine, then bring to the boil. Reduce the heat to low and simmer uncovered for at least 1 hour but for a richer sauce and more tender beef mince simmer for 2 hours, stirring occasionally. The mixture should thicken and become rich in flavour. Add more water as needed if it becomes too dry. Season with salt and pepper to taste.

5 Add the frozen peas and stir to combine. They will thaw in the hot filling. Spoon the filling mixture into an 8 cup capacity ovenproof dish and set aside to cool slightly, so the mashed potato doesn't sink into the filling.

6 Preheat the oven to 180°C.

7 To make the topping, place the potato into a large saucepan and cover with cold water. Generously season with salt. Bring to the boil over medium-high heat and cook for about 15 minutes, or until a knife can easily pierce through the potato.

8 Drain the potatoes and return to the pan. Add the cold butter and mash the potato until smooth and creamy. Add more butter if desired. Gradually add the warm milk, a little at a time, to loosen the mash and make it fluffy. Whisking the potatoes will help incorporate air, making them extra light and smooth. Season with salt to taste.

9 Spoon the mashed potato over the filling in an even layer. For a rustic look, use a fork to create texture on the top of the mashed potatoes.

10 To make the crumb topping, combine the ingredients in a small bowl. Sprinkle evenly over the mashed potato.

11 Stand the dish on an oven tray. Bake for 15 minutes, or until the topping is golden brown and the filling is bubbling up around the edges. Set aside for 5 minutes to cool slightly before serving.

Barbecue
Glazed Ribs

Barbecue Glazed Ribs

One thing that I love is barbecued meats. One thing I don't have is a smoker or the knowledge
to use one. If you're in the same position or really just want some ribs, this is the recipe for you.
This easy technique will leave you with perfectly soft, glazed pork ribs all from your oven.

SERVES 2–4
PREP TIME 10 minutes
COOK TIME 2½–3½ hours

1.2 kg rack pork baby back ribs
garlic powder, to taste
homemade barbecue sauce
    (page 211)

1   Preheat the oven to 150°C. Pat the ribs dry with paper towel. Using
    another paper towel, remove the membrane from the underside of the
    ribs. I find it easiest to pull the membrane away slightly from the shorter
    end and then holding tightly with paper towel pull towards the opposite
    end to remove.

2   Lay ribs on a large sheet of foil, then season generously with garlic
    powder, salt and freshly ground black pepper. Enclose tightly in the foil.
    Place onto a wire rack set over a rimmed baking tray.

3   Cook for 2–3 hours (the longer time is better, if you have it), until a knife
    easily pierces the meat, or the internal temperature reaches 90°C when
    tested with a meat thermometer.

4   Take the ribs out of the oven and increase the heat to 190°C. Open up the
    foil and brush a good layer of barbecue sauce over the ribs. Return to
    the oven for another 20–30 minutes, brushing with more barbecue sauce
    every 10 minutes until you have a deep, dark glaze.

5   Set aside to rest for 5–10 minutes before serving.

Coq au Vin

The very French name might scare you into thinking that this will be difficult to make but 'ne sois pas un lâche' (that's French for 'don't be a coward'). Coq au vin was on the menu the entire time I worked for Pascal and it was always a fight between us to be the one to scrape the leftover gravy out of the pot with bread.

SERVES 4
PREP TIME 15 minutes
COOK TIME 45–50 minutes

1 tablespoon olive oil
4 chicken marylands (joined thigh
   and drumstick)
100 g bacon or speck, diced
1 brown onion, chopped
2 carrots, sliced
2 stalk celery, diced
2 cloves garlic, crushed
250 g button mushrooms, sliced
1 cup (250 ml) dry red wine (like pinot
   noir or shiraz)
1 cup (250 ml) chicken stock
1–2 sprigs fresh thyme (or 1 teaspoon
   dried thyme)
1 dried bay leaf
fresh parsley, to serve

1. Heat the olive oil in a large, heavy-based pan (like a dutch oven) over medium-high heat. Season the chicken with salt and pepper. Brown the chicken pieces, skin-side down first, for about 5–7 minutes, until golden brown on all sides. Remove the chicken and set aside.

2. In the same pan, add the bacon or speck. Cook, stirring occasionally, for 3–4 minutes, until crispy. Add the onion, carrot and celery. Cook for another 5 minutes, stirring occasionally, until softened. Add the garlic and mushrooms and cook for 2–3 minutes until the mushrooms release their moisture and start to brown.

3. Pour in the red wine, scraping the bottom of the pan to release any brown bits. Add the chicken stock, thyme, bay leaf, and a pinch of salt and freshly ground black pepper. Bring to a simmer.

4. Return the chicken to the pan, skin-side up. Reduce the heat to low, cover with a lid, and simmer gently for 30–40 minutes, until the chicken is cooked through and tender. (If needed, add a little extra stock or water during cooking to keep the sauce from reducing too much.)

5. Taste the sauce and adjust the seasoning with salt and pepper if needed. Remove the bay leaf and thyme sprigs. Serve the chicken with the sauce spooned over the top, sprinkled with parsley.

Slow-
cooked
Harissa
Lamb
Shoulder

Slow-cooked Harissa Lamb Shoulder

Picture this: you get home and see the slow cooker on the kitchen bench and you
feel defeated until you realise it contains a slow-cooked harissa lamb shoulder!
I think this spicy, slow-cooked wonder can improve even the worst days.

SERVES 6–8
PREP TIME 15 minutes (plus marinating time, ideally overnight)
COOK TIME 3–4 hours (oven) or 6–8 hours (slow cooker)

1.5–2 kg lamb shoulder (bone-in,
  with fat cap)

OVEN INGREDIENTS (if using)
1 large brown onion, roughly
  chopped
2 carrots, cut into large chunks
2 sticks celery, cut into large chunks
2 cups (500 ml) beef or chicken stock
  (or water)

HARISSA MARINADE
¼ cup (60 ml) olive oil
¼ cup (75 g) harissa paste (or to
  taste, depending on your spice
  preference)
3 cloves garlic, crushed
2 tablespoons lemon juice
1 tablespoon honey (optional,
  to balance the heat)
1 tablespoon ground cumin
1 tablespoon ground coriander
1 teaspoon ground cinnamon
1 teaspoon smoked paprika
½ teaspoon ground turmeric

1   To make the harissa marinade, whisk the olive oil, harissa paste, garlic, lemon juice, honey (if using) and spices in a bowl. Season generously with salt and freshly ground black pepper. Taste the marinade to ensure it has a good balance of heat, sweetness and spice. Adjust the harissa or honey if needed.

2   Pat the lamb shoulder dry with paper towels. Place the lamb into a large shallow dish and pour the harissa marinade over the lamb. Wearing gloves to avoid the chilli burning your hands, rub the marinade into the meat, ensuring it's evenly coated. Cover the dish, and marinate in the fridge for at least 4 hours, or preferably overnight. This will allow the flavours to infuse deeply into the lamb.

3   Set a slow cooker to low. Place the lamb and stock into the slow cooker. Cover and cook on low for 6–8 hours, or until the lamb is incredibly tender and falls apart when pulled with a fork.

4   Alternatively, you can cook in the oven. Preheat oven to 160°C. Heat a large flame-proof and oven-proof dish (like a dutch oven) on the stovetop over medium heat. Add a splash of olive oil, then sear the lamb shoulder for about 3–4 minutes per side, until browned all over. This helps to lock in the flavour.

5   Arrange the onion, carrot and celery in a roasting pan and sit the seared lamb on top. Pour the stock (or water) around the lamb. Cover tightly with foil and roast for 3–4 hours, or until the lamb is tender and pulls apart easily with a fork. Check the lamb halfway through cooking and add a bit more stock or water if necessary to keep the vegetables from burning.

6   Remove lamb from the cooking vessel and let it rest for 10 minutes before carving. The lamb should be so tender that it easily pulls apart. If you like, strain the cooking liquid and serve it as a sauce, or leave the vegetables in for a rustic presentation. Serve the lamb with the roasted vegetables (if you have them) and a drizzle of the cooking juices. You could also pull the lamb from the bone and use it as the filling for a wrap with garlic sauce (page 205), pickles and fresh vegetables.

Meat Pie

I'm here to settle the debate about who has better pies and I'm sorry to say that the meat pies in New Zealand really are just better. When I stayed in Queenstown a few years ago I had a Fergbaker meat pie every day and it's still something I think about often. My pie recipe isn't reminiscent or trying to replicate that at all because it's futile, but this pie has everything that I think makes a great pie. A shortcrust base filled with pull-apart beef, crispy speck and a rich gravy baked top with a buttery, flaky crust.

SERVES 6–8
PREP TIME 30 minutes
COOK TIME about 3 hours

200 g speck, skin off, diced
1 kg beef chuck steak, cubed
1 brown onion, thinly sliced
3 cloves garlic, crushed
1½ tablespoons tomato paste
½ bunch thyme, leaves chopped
1 tablespoon beef stock powder
　(or 1 litre real beef stock)
1½ tablespoons Worcestershire
　sauce
2 teaspoons cornflour
50 g low-moisture mozzarella,
　shredded
1 sheet frozen shortcrust pastry,
　just thawed
1 sheet frozen puff pastry,
　just thawed
1 egg, lightly beaten

1　Heat a large, heavy-based pan (like a dutch oven) over medium-low heat. Add the speck and cook for 5–10 minutes, stirring occasionally, until the fat is rendered out and the speck becomes crispy. Remove the speck from the pot, leaving the rendered fat behind. Set the speck aside for later.

2　Season the beef generously with salt and freshly ground black pepper. Increase the heat to medium-high and sear the beef cubes in batches, browning them on all sides to develop a deep brown crust. Transfer to a plate and set aside.

3　Reduce the heat to medium. Add the onion and a pinch of salt. Sauté for 3–5 minutes, until softened and translucent. Add the garlic and cook for 30 seconds, just to release its aroma.

4　Push the onion and garlic to the sides of the pot to create a space in the centre. Add the tomato paste and cook for 1 minute, to deepen the flavour. Stir in the thyme and mix well with the onion and garlic.

5　Return the beef and speck to the pan. Pour in just enough water to cover the meat (about 1 litre). Add the beef stock powder and Worcestershire sauce. Stir to combine and dissolve the stock powder. Bring the mixture to a simmer, then reduce the heat to low. Cover with a lid and cook gently for 1½–2 hours, until the beef is pull apart tender.

6　After the meat is soft enough to squish between your fingers, prepare a slurry by mixing the cornflour with ½ cup (125 ml) water until smooth. Stir into the simmering stew and cook for a few minutes, until the sauce thickens. Season with salt and freshly ground black pepper to taste.

7　Transfer the filling into a baking dish, spreading it out evenly. Place the dish in the fridge or freezer to cool completely (this step is important to prevent soggy pastry).

8 Preheat the oven to 180°C. Grease a 23 cm pie tin with oil. Line the tin with the shortcrust pastry, trimming off any excess dough around the edges. Spoon the cooled meat filling into the pastry-lined tin, pressing it down flat. Sprinkle the shredded mozzarella evenly over the top, leaving a gap around the edge for the lid to join to the base.

9 Brush the edges of the shortcrust pastry with a little beaten egg. Place the puff pastry over the pie and crimp the edges with a fork to seal. Trim any excess pastry. Cut a small vent in the centre of the pie to allow steam to escape during baking. Brush the top of the pie with more egg wash for a golden, glossy finish.

10 Bake the pie for 30–40 minutes, or until the puff pastry is golden and crisp. Set aside for 10–15 minutes before serving, to let the filling set.

11 Serve with a side of mashed potato and gravy, a simple garden salad or just load it up with the sauce of your choice (I'm a tomato sauce guy) and tuck in.

Spaghetti and Meatballs

Spaghetti and meatballs is another childhood favourite of mine. I knew I was in for a treat when I saw Mum grating mountains of parmesan and rolling the pork and veal mince. I really didn't have a clue what was good for me as a kid though – the 'dry' meatballs were my favourite because I was an idiot with no clue what else was out there. Now I know all about the 'wet' ones, cooked for hours in a rich tomato sauce.

SERVES 4–6
PREP TIME 30 minutes
COOK TIME 1 hour 15 minutes–
   1 hour 45 minutes

300 g dried spaghetti
finely grated parmesan, to serve

TOMATO SAUCE
2 tablespoons olive oil
1 brown onion, finely diced
3 cloves garlic, crushed
2 teaspoons dried chilli flakes
4 cups (1 litre) passata
1 tablespoon dried oregano

MEATBALLS
100 g day-old bread, preferably
   a baguette/French stick
150 ml milk
500 g pork mince
500 g veal mince
1 egg
80 g finely grated parmesan
1 teaspoon ground black pepper
3 cloves garlic, finely grated
½ cup flat-leaf parsley, chopped
1 tablespoon oregano leaves, finely
   chopped

If you end up with any leftovers (I don't see that happening) they are perfect on a sandwich or pizza the next day. I actually think that these meatballs are much better over the next few days, after having time to sit in the rich sauce and soak up all the flavours.

1. To make the tomato sauce, heat the olive oil in a large saucepan over medium heat. Add the onion and cook for about 2 minutes, stirring occasionally, until softened.

2. Add the garlic and chilli flakes, and cook for another 2 minutes, stirring constantly, until fragrant.

3. Pour in the passata. Fill each empty passata bottle about one-third full with water. Give the bottles a good shake to loosen any leftover sauce, then pour the water into the pan.

4. Stir in the dried oregano and a generous pinch of salt. Bring the sauce to a simmer, then reduce the heat to low and let it simmer gently, uncovered, for about 20 minutes, while you prepare the meatballs.

5. For the meatballs, soak the bread in milk for 10 minutes. Gently squeeze out any excess milk.

6. Preheat the grill to high heat. In a large mixing bowl, combine the soaked bread, pork mince, veal mince, egg, parmesan, pepper, garlic, parsley and oregano. Use your hands to mix everything together for about 5 minutes, until the mixture is smooth.

7. Wet your hands lightly to prevent sticking, then shape the mixture into 16 even-sized meatballs.

8. Arrange the meatballs on a greased baking tray and cook under the grill for 10 minutes, turning occasionally to brown evenly.

9. Gently add the meatballs to the simmering sauce. Cover the pan and cook in the sauce for at least 30 minutes, but the longer they simmer, the more tender and flavourful they will become (1–2 hours is ideal).

10. While the meatballs cook, bring a large pot of salted water to the boil. Add the spaghetti and cook according to the package instructions (usually about 9–11 minutes) until al dente.

11. Drain the spaghetti, toss with a few spoonfuls of the sauce.

12. Serve the meatballs on top of the spaghetti with a generous amount of the sauce and a sprinkle of parmesan.

Chicken Cacciatore

When I said that my dad likes to experiment with his cooking, I meant that he would
do strange things like putting blueberries into his cacciatore. Luckily this isn't my dad's
recipe but I do admire his bravery, even if his choices of ingredients are insane.

SERVES 4
PREP TIME 15 minutes
COOK TIME 1 hour 15 minutes

2 tablespoons olive oil
4 bone-in, skin-on chicken thighs
1 large brown onion, finely chopped
1 red capsicum, sliced
2 cloves garlic, crushed
½ cup (125 ml) dry white wine
   (optional)
400 g can crushed tomatoes
½ cup (125 ml) chicken stock
   (or water)
¼ cup (40 g) kalamata olives,
   pitted and halved
1 tablespoon capers, drained
2 teaspoons dried oregano
1 teaspoon dried basil
½ teaspoon dried chilli flakes
   (optional)
fresh parsley, chopped (for garnish)

1. Heat 1 tablespoon of the oil in a large, deep frying pan (or dutch oven) over medium-high heat. Season the chicken thighs with salt and pepper on both sides. Add the chicken to the pan, skin-side down, and cook for 5–7 minutes per side, until golden brown. You may need to do this in batches to avoid overcrowding the pan. Transfer the chicken to a plate and set aside.

2. Heat the remaining oil in the pan. Add the onion and capsicum. Sauté for 5–7 minutes, stirring occasionally, until softened. Add the garlic and cook for 30 seconds, until fragrant.

3. Pour in the white wine and stir, scraping up any browned bits from the bottom of the pan. Simmer for 2–3 minutes until reduced slightly. If you're not using wine, just proceed to the next step.

4. Add the tomatoes, stock, olives, capers, oregano, basil and chilli flakes (if using). Stir to combine. Return the chicken to the pan, skin-side up, making sure the chicken is partially submerged in the sauce. Bring the sauce to a simmer, then reduce the heat to low. Cover the pan and cook for 40 minutes, or until the chicken is fully cooked through.

5. Season with salt and pepper to taste. Sprinkle with parsley just before serving.

6. Serve with crusty bread to soak up the sauce, over pasta (spaghetti or penne), or with mashed potatoes.

CHAPTER 4

A Little Sweet Treat

Choc-chip and Walnut Banana Loaf

Banana bread really is just the best. Hungry? Have some banana bread.
Sad? Have some banana bread. Make this banana bread on Sunday
so you have at least one thing to look forward to each day.

SERVES 8–10
PREP TIME 15 minutes
COOK TIME about 1 hour

3 ripe bananas
125 g unsalted butter, at room
   temperature, chopped
1 cup (220 g) brown sugar
   (or caster sugar)
2 eggs
1 teaspoon vanilla extract
1½ cups (225 g) self-raising flour
½ teaspoon bicarbonate of soda
½ teaspoon ground cinnamon
¼ teaspoon salt
½ cup (95 g) chocolate chips
½ cup (50 g) walnuts, roughly
   chopped

1. Preheat the oven to 180°C. Grease and line a loaf pan (23 cm × 13 cm) with baking paper, or grease and dust lightly with flour.

2. Use a fork to mash the bananas, leaving a few lumps for texture (or mash until smooth if you don't like lumps).

3. In a large bowl, use an electric mixer to beat the butter and sugar for 3–4 minutes or until light and fluffy. Add the eggs one at a time, beating well after each addition. Mix in the vanilla extract.

4. In a separate bowl, whisk together the flour, bicarb soda, cinnamon and salt.

5. Add the mashed bananas to the butter mixture and stir until combined. Fold in the dry ingredients until just combined – be careful not to over-mix. Gently fold in the chocolate chips and walnuts.

6. Pour the batter into the prepared pan and smooth the top with a spatula. Bake for about 1 hour, until a skewer or toothpick inserted into the centre comes out clean (or with just a few moist crumbs). If the top is browning too quickly, cover loosely with foil and continue baking.

7. Cool in the pan for about 10 minutes, then remove from the pan and cool completely on a wire rack.

These can be easily turned into cupcakes. Line a 12-cup (80 ml capacity) muffin tin with paper liners and divide the mixture evenly between them. Bake for 20–25 minutes or until a skewer inserted into the centre comes out clean.

Proper
Chocolate
Mousse

Proper Chocolate Mousse

I think chocolate mousse is the bread and butter of desserts, incredibly simple but when done right it steals the show. This chocolate mousse is as simple as it gets and it's guaranteed to leave your guests (or yourself) wanting more!

SERVES 6–8
PREP TIME 20 minutes
COOK TIME 10 minutes plus 2 hours chilling

½ teaspoon powdered gelatine
2 teaspoons cold water
300 g milk chocolate
600 g heavy cream, divided into 150 g and 450 g
½ teaspoon vanilla extract

To create the swirl on the inside of the glass, scoop some of the ganache with a spoon whilst still warm and runny. Then whilst holding the spoon still in one hand, swirl the glass with your other hand to create the pattern on the inside of the glass.

1   In a small cup, sprinkle ½ teaspoon of powdered gelatine evenly over 2 teaspoons of cold water. Let it sit for 5–10 minutes to fully absorb the water and swell (this is called blooming). Make sure you sprinkle it evenly – don't just dump it in a pile, or it will clump.

2   Chop the milk chocolate finely and melt it gently over a bain-marie (hot-water bath) or in short microwave bursts, stirring frequently, until fully smooth. Set aside to cool slightly.

3   In a small saucepan, heat 150 g of the cream until it just starts to simmer (do not boil).

4   Once the cream is hot, remove it from the heat. Add the bloomed gelatine (it will look like a firm gel) into the hot cream. Stir gently until completely dissolved. If you see any bits that don't melt, you can gently reheat over low heat, but avoid boiling – gelatine weakens if overheated.

5   Gradually pour the hot cream with gelatine over the melted chocolate in three additions, stirring gently with a spatula or whisk, creating a smooth, glossy ganache.

6   Combine the remaining 450 g of cream and vanilla extract and whip until soft peaks form – it should be light, fluffy, and barely hold its shape.

7   When the chocolate ganache has cooled to around 35–38°C (lukewarm), fold in the whipped cream gently in three stages, keeping as much air in the mousse as possible.

8   Immediately portion the mousse into glasses, bowls, or a serving container. Refrigerate for around 2 hours to softly set.

Pear and
Almond Tart

Pear and Almond Tart

My girlfriend, Abbie, told me that this recipe HAD to be in the book. I think it's clear that it's her favourite and there's a good reason for that – it's really good.

SWEET SHORTCRUST PASTRY
1 cup (150 g) plain flour
25 g icing sugar
75 g unsalted butter, chilled and cubed
1 egg yolk
2–3 tablespoons chilled water

ALMOND CREAM (FRANGIPANE)
100 g unsalted butter, at room temperature, chopped
100 g caster sugar
2 eggs
100 g almond meal
1 teaspoon vanilla extract

FILLING
410 g can sliced pears in juice, drained
2 tablespoons apricot jam (optional)

1 To make the pastry, combine the flour, icing sugar and butter in a food processor. Pulse in short bursts until the mixture resembles breadcrumbs. Add the egg yolk and pulse again until the dough starts to come together. Add the water, 1 tablespoon at a time (you may not need it all), until the dough forms a ball. Turn the dough out onto a lightly floured surface and knead gently. Flatten it into a disc, wrap in plastic wrap, and refrigerate for minimum 30 minutes, or ideally until completely cold.

2 For the almond cream, use an electric mixer to beat the softened butter and caster sugar in a mixing bowl together until light and fluffy. Beat in the eggs one at a time, ensuring each is fully incorporated before adding the next. Stir in the ground almonds and vanilla extract, mixing until smooth. The almond cream should be smooth and creamy. Set aside.

3 Preheat the oven to 180°C.

4 Remove the pastry from the fridge for about 20 minutes, to soften slightly. On a lightly floured surface, roll out the pastry to about 3 mm thickness. Use it to line a 23 cm–25 cm loose-based tart tin, pressing it gently into the edges. Trim any excess pastry.

5 To prevent a soggy base, it's best to blind bake the pastry. Use a fork to poke small holes in the pastry (this is called docking), to help it to bake more evenly and prevent air bubbles from forming (these can grow really big and ruin everything). Line the tart shell with baking paper and fill with baking weights, dried beans or rice. Bake for 10–12 minutes, until the edges are lightly golden. Remove the paper and weights, then bake for another 5 minutes to cook the base.

6 Spoon the almond cream into the tart shell and smooth it out evenly with a spatula. Lay the pears on top of the almond cream, arranging them in a spiral pattern or however you want, (this is your masterpiece).

7   Place the tart back into the oven and bake for 30–35 minutes, or until
    the almond cream is golden and set. Check the tart around 25 minutes
    to ensure it doesn't over-brown. If necessary, cover the edges with foil
    to protect the pastry.

8   To make a glaze (optional), heat the apricot jam in a small saucepan over
    low heat until melted. Brush the jam over the pears and almond cream to
    give the tart a beautiful glossy finish. Allow the tart to cool in the tin for
    10 minutes before transferring it to a wire rack to cool completely.

9   Slice the tart into wedges and serve as a delicious dessert, ideally with
    a dollop of whipped cream or a scoop of vanilla ice cream.

Cold ingredients keep the butter solid, creating a flaky texture as it steams during
baking, and also slows gluten development for a more tender, non-greasy pastry.
This makes the dough easier to handle and helps to hold its shape.

Single Serve Self-saucing Pudding

Self-saucing pudding is exactly what I want when I'm suggesting 'a little something sweet'. It's perfect for a late night craving and can be ready in about 30 minutes, plus it feels like a little magic is happening with the whole 'self-saucing' aspect. I never believe it will work and then it just does.

SERVES 1
PREP TIME 10 minutes
COOK TIME 25–30 minutes

30 g unsalted butter, melted
2 tablespoons caster sugar
2 tablespoons brown sugar
½ teaspoon vanilla extract
1 egg
40 g plain flour
2 tablespoons cocoa powder
½ teaspoon baking powder
¼ cup (60 ml) milk

SAUCE
2 tablespoons brown sugar
1 tablespoon cocoa powder
100 ml hot water (or strong coffee
    for a deeper flavour)

1 Preheat the oven to 180°C. Grease a 175 ml ramekin with a little butter or oil.

2 In a medium bowl, whisk together the melted butter, caster sugar, brown sugar and vanilla extract until fully combined. Beat in the egg until the mixture is smooth. Sift the flour, cocoa powder, baking powder and a pinch of salt into the bowl, then fold gently into the batter. Add the milk and stir until the batter is smooth and well combined.

3 Spoon the mixture into the prepared ramekin and smooth the surface. Stand the ramekin on a baking tray.

4 To make the sauce, mix the brown sugar and cocoa powder together. Sprinkle evenly over the top of the batter in the ramekin. Carefully pour the hot water (or coffee) over the top. Do not stir – this is what will create the self-saucing effect as the pudding bakes.

5 Bake for 25–30 minutes, until the top is set and slightly cracked, but the centre remains soft. The sauce will form at the bottom, and the top will be cakey.

6 Let the pudding cool for a few minutes before serving. You can top with a scoop of vanilla ice cream, whipped cream, or a dusting of icing sugar for extra indulgence.

Bonne Ma
Raspberry-Lightly

Jam-filled
Donut Balls

Jam-filled Donut Balls

If you've finished dinner an hour ago, are craving something sweet and aren't afraid of hot oil, you should definitely make these donut balls. Little fried dough balls filled with jam and rolled in sugar, so good and also so easy.

MAKES 12–16 donut balls
PREP TIME 15 minutes
COOK TIME 10–15 minutes

200 g self-raising flour
200 g Greek yoghurt
4–5 tablespoons raspberry jam
(or your preferred jam)
vegetable oil, for frying
50 g caster sugar

1 Put the flour and yoghurt into a mixing bowl and stir until it forms a soft dough. If the dough feels too sticky, add a little extra flour, but it should remain soft and slightly tacky.

2 Divide the dough into small pieces and roll each piece into a small ball (about 2–3 cm in diameter). Using your finger or a small spoon, make a small indentation in the center of each ball to create a pocket. Be careful not to go all the way through. Fill the indentation with about 1 teaspoon raspberry jam. Gently seal the dough around the jam and roll it back into a ball shape. Make sure the jam is fully enclosed to prevent it from leaking during frying.

3 Half-fill a deep fryer or large deep pan with vegetable oil and heat to 180°C. Make sure there's enough oil to submerge the donut balls completely. Fry the balls in batches for 3–4 minutes, turning occasionally to ensure they cook evenly and turn golden brown on all sides. Be cautious not to overcrowd the fryer or pan, because this will lower the oil temperature and result in uneven cooking. Use a slotted spoon to remove the donut balls from the oil and place them on paper towel to drain excess oil.

4 While the donut balls are still warm, roll them in caster sugar to coat them evenly. This will give them a nice sweet crunch on the outside.

Pascal's Raspberry and White Chocolate Muffins

Pascal would make these muffins every morning, hours before I even rocked up late to work and I always wanted to steal one from the tin. I would hope that he missed the muffin liner, getting batter on the muffin tray that I could eat. These muffins are so good that I had to steal this recipe from him – sorry, boss.

MAKES 12
PREP TIME 20 minutes
COOK TIME 45 minutes

1 cup (220 g) caster sugar
4 eggs
2 cups (600 ml) cream
1 teaspoon vanilla extract (optional)
3⅓ cups (500 g) self-raising flour
1 cup (190 g) white chocolate chips
1 cup (200 g) frozen raspberries

RASPBERRY COULIS SWIRL
1 cup (150 g) frozen raspberries
½ cup (110 g) raw sugar
juice of ½ lime
1 teaspoon gelatine powder

These muffins can be stored in an airtight container at room temperature for up to 3 days, or in the fridge for up to a week. They can also be frozen for up to 2 months. Simply wrap them individually in plastic wrap and then place them in a freezer bag. Reheat in the microwave or oven when ready to serve.

1   For the raspberry coulis swirl, combine the raspberries, raw sugar and lime juice in a small saucepan. Cook the mixture over medium heat for 15–20 minutes, stirring occasionally, until the raspberries break down and the sugar dissolves. The mixture should become syrupy. Once the raspberry mixture has thickened, sprinkle in the gelatine powder and stir to combine. Simmer for another 1–2 minutes to dissolve the gelatine. Remove from heat and blend the mixture with an immersion blender (or regular blender) until smooth. Set aside to cool while you prepare the muffin batter.

2   Preheat the oven to 180°C and line 2 large (1.2 L capacity) muffin trays with paper liners. In a large bowl, whisk together the sugar and eggs until well combined. Add the cream, a pinch of salt, and vanilla extract (if using), stirring until smooth and combined. Gradually add the flour, stirring until fully incorporated and there are no lumps in the batter. Gently fold in the white chocolate chips and frozen raspberries, making sure everything is evenly distributed in the batter.

3   Spoon the muffin batter into the lined muffin tray, filling each cup about ¾ full. Transfer the raspberry coulis to a piping bag fitted with a 3mm nozzle. Pipe about 1 tablespoon of the coulis onto the top of each muffin. Take a skewer or a knife and gently swirl the coulis into the batter, creating a marbled effect.

4   Bake for 10 minutes. Cover the tray loosely with foil to prevent over-browning and bake for 10–15 minutes more, until risen and golden brown. Test by inserting a bamboo skewer into the centre of a muffin – if it comes out clean, the muffins are done.

5   Allow to cool in the tray for 5 minutes before transferring to a wire rack to cool completely.

Pascal's Raspberry and White Chocolate Muffins

Apple and Rhubarb Crumble Tart

My grandma would make apple and rhubarb crumble for family dinners, and it would always make me so happy to hear that it was on the menu. She would pick the rhubarb from her garden and stew it with apples until it was soft but still held together. I think this is the perfect paring of sweet and sour, especially with green apples!

SERVES 6–8
PREP TIME 30 minutes plus
   30 minutes chilling
COOK TIME 1 hour

SWEET SHORTCRUST PASTRY
200 g plain flour
100 g unsalted butter, chilled
   and cubed
50 g caster sugar
1 egg yolk
2–3 tablespoons chilled water

APPLE AND RHUBARB FILLING
300 g granny smith apples (about 2),
   peeled, cored and chopped
250 g rhubarb, chopped into 2 cm
   pieces
100 g caster sugar
1 tablespoon lemon juice
½ teaspoon ground cinnamon
1 tablespoon cornflour

CRUMBLE TOPPING
100 g plain flour
50 g rolled oats
100 g unsalted butter, chilled and
   cubed
75 g brown sugar
½ teaspoon ground cinnamon

1   To make the pastry, in a large bowl, rub the flour and butter together until the mixture resembles breadcrumbs. Stir in the sugar, then add the egg yolk. Mix until just combined. If the dough is too dry, add the water, a tablespoon at a time, until the dough comes together. Gather into a ball, then press out to a disc shape. Wrap the dough in plastic wrap and chill it in the fridge for at least 30 minutes.

2   Preheat the oven to 180°C.

3   Roll the dough on a lightly floured surface until it's about 3–4mm thick. Carefully line a 22 cm–24 cm loose-based tart tin with the pastry, pressing it gently into the corners. Trim off any excess pastry hanging over the edges.

4   Line the pastry with baking paper and fill with baking weights, dried beans or rice. Stand the tin on a baking tray and bake for 10–12 minutes, until the edges are lightly golden. Remove the paper and weights, then bake for an additional 5 minutes to cook the base. Set aside to cool.

5   For the filling, combine the apples and rhubarb in a large bowl. Add the sugar, lemon juice and cinnamon. Stir gently to coat the fruit. Dissolve the cornflour in 1 tablespoon of water, then stir it into the fruit mixture. The cornflour will help thicken the juices as the fruit cooks. Transfer the mixture to a saucepan and cook over medium heat for about 5 minutes, stirring occasionally, until the fruit starts to soften and release its juices. Remove from heat and set aside to cool slightly.

6   To make the topping, combine the flour, oats, butter, sugar and cinnamon. Using your fingertips, rub the butter into the dry ingredients until the mixture resembles coarse crumbs. You should have a nice, chunky crumble topping.

7   Spoon the slightly cooled apple and rhubarb filling into the par-baked tart shell, spreading it out evenly. Sprinkle the crumble topping evenly over the fruit filling, covering it generously.

8   Bake for 25–30 minutes, or until the crumble topping is golden brown and crispy, and the filling is bubbling. Allow the tart to cool for 10–15 minutes before serving. The filling will thicken as it cools.

9   Serve with a scoop of vanilla ice cream or custard. Trust me, this will be the best crumble of your life.

Crème Caramel

This is a dessert that can be scary to make because the eggs can curdle if you're not careful, but when you get it right it's so silky smooth and delicious. Make sure to pay really close attention when baking – it will be ready when it is just set but still wobbles slightly when gently shaken. It will continue to cook when you take it out of the oven.

SERVES 6–8
PREP TIME 20 minutes
COOK TIME 50–60 minutes plus
4 hours or overnight chilling

CARAMEL
150 g caster sugar

CUSTARD
2 cups (500 ml) full-fat milk
1 vanilla bean (seeds scraped,
pod reserved)
4 eggs
4 egg yolks
100 g caster sugar

Remove the cake tin from the roasting pan and allow it to cool to room temperature, then move to the fridge for at least 4 hours but preferably overnight to fully set. To serve, run a knife around the edges of the cake tin to loosen the custard from the sides. Carefully invert the tin onto a large rimmed plate. The caramel will flow over the custard, creating a beautiful sauce.

1   Preheat the oven to 160°C. Have a 22 cm–24 cm round cake tin ready on hand.

2   To make the caramel, put the sugar into a medium saucepan and add 1½ tablespoons water. Heat over medium heat, stirring gently until the sugar dissolves. Once dissolved, stop stirring and let the mixture bubble. Cook for 5–7 minutes or until the sugar turns a deep amber colour, being careful not to burn it.

3   Immediately pour the hot caramel into the cake tin and gently swirl it to coat the bottom evenly (take care as the tin will get hot). Set aside for the caramel to cool and harden.

4   For the custard, combine the milk with the scraped vanilla seeds and pod in a medium saucepan. Heat over medium heat until it just begins to simmer, stirring occasionally. Once it starts to steam and small bubbles appear around the edges, remove from heat.

5   Let the vanilla pod steep in the milk for 10–15 minutes to infuse the flavour. After steeping, discard the vanilla pod and set the milk aside.

6   In a large mixing bowl, whisk together the eggs, yolks, sugar and a pinch of salt until smooth and slightly lightened in colour.

7   Gradually pour the warm vanilla-infused milk into the egg mixture, stirring continuously to prevent curdling. Once fully combined, strain the custard through a fine mesh sieve into another clean bowl or large jug to remove any cooked egg bits.

8   Pour the custard mixture into the cake tin over the hardened caramel (make sure the caramel has hardened before pouring the custard).

9   Place the cake tin into a large roasting pan. Add hot water to the roasting pan around the cake tin, ensuring the water comes about halfway up the sides of the cake tin (this is the bain-marie or water bath method, which ensures gentle cooking).

10 Carefully transfer the pan to the oven and bake for 50–60 minutes, or until the custard is just set but still slightly wobbly in the centre. The custard should jiggle gently when tapped but not slosh. To test doneness, insert a thin knife into the centre – it should come out clean, but the custard should still have a slight jiggle.

Two Ingredient Ice Cream

This ice cream base is practically fool proof. Use this as a guide and have your way with it: add any flavours and mix-ins to make it YOUR ice cream.

SERVES 6–8 servings
PREP TIME 15 minutes plus at least 6 hours freezing time

2 cups (500 ml) thickened cream (full-fat)
395 g can sweetened condensed milk

1 Use an electric mixer to whip the cream in a large bowl until stiff peaks form. This should take about 3–5 minutes. Be careful not to over-whip it because the cream can split, resulting in a lumpy mess that won't come together.

2 Gently fold the sweetened condensed milk into the whipped cream. Fold in your choice of mix-in now.

3 Transfer the mixture into a loaf pan, airtight container, or any freezer-safe dish. Smooth the top with a spatula.

4 Cover the container with plastic wrap or a lid and freeze for at least 6 hours, or until completely firm.

MIX-INS

These can be as basic as just a dash of vanilla extract, some chocolate chips or fresh fruit. If you like, use one of the fancier mix-ins below.

MINT CHOC CHIP

Add 1 teaspoon peppermint extract and 1–2 drops green food colouring when you have almost finished whipping the cream. Beat in briefly to mix through. Fold 100 g finely chopped chocolate (or chocolate chips) through at the end of step 2.

SALTED CARAMEL SWIRL

In a saucepan, heat 100 g caster sugar over medium heat until it melts then turns golden brown. Stir in 60 g butter and ¼ cup (60 ml) cream and continue to cook for another 2 minutes. Remove from heat and stir in a pinch of sea salt. Transfer to a bowl to cool completely. Transfer half the ice cream base into the loaf pan. Drizzle the salted caramel sauce over the ice cream base in a few lines. Using a knife or spoon, gently swirl the caramel for a marbled effect. Don't over mix – you want ribbons of caramel, not fully combined! Repeat with the remaining ice cream base and salted caramel sauce.

CHOC CHIP COOKIE DOUGH

Preheat the oven to 180°C. Spread 125 g plain flour onto a baking tray and bake for 7 minutes, to kill any bacteria. Cool completely. In a bowl, beat 100 g softened unsalted butter and 100 g brown sugar together until creamy. Add 1 teaspoon vanilla extract and a pinch of salt and mix well. Stir in the flour until the mixture comes together into a dough. Fold in 50 g chocolate chips. Roll the cookie dough into small balls, about the size of a marble (roughly 1 cm diameter). Place them on a baking tray lined with baking paper and chill in the freezer for about 30 minutes, or until firm. This will make the cookie dough chunks perfect for mixing into the ice cream.

Pear and Raspberry Turnovers

I couldn't have a dessert chapter without using puff pastry at least once,
and these turnovers are such an easy and delicious pastry to make.
You can make the filling in the time it takes to pre-heat the oven.

MAKES 8
PREP TIME 15 minutes
COOK TIME 30 minutes

2 ripe pears, peeled, cored and
   diced
150 g frozen raspberries
2 tablespoons caster sugar
1 teaspoon lemon juice
1 tablespoon cornflour
2 sheets frozen puff pastry,
   just thawed
1 egg
icing sugar, to dust

1. Preheat the oven to 200°C and line a baking tray with baking paper.

2. In a medium saucepan, combine the pears, raspberries, sugar and lemon juice. Cook over medium heat for 5–7 minutes, stirring occasionally, until the pears soften and the raspberries break down. If the mixture looks too runny, stir the cornflour with 1 tablespoon water until smooth, then add to the fruit mixture. Continue cooking for another 1–2 minutes until the filling thickens. Transfer to a bowl to cool.

3. Divide each sheet of puff pastry into 4 squares. Spoon one-eighth of the filling, just under half a cup, into the centre of a square, allowing enough room for the pastry to be folded over itself.

4. Fold the corners of the pastry over to create a triangle shape, enclosing the filling. Press the edges together with your fingers, then crimp with a fork to seal tightly. Place onto the prepared tray and repeat with remaining filling and pastry.

5. Beat the egg in a small bowl and brush it lightly over the top of each turnover to give them a golden, glossy finish when baked (you can add 1 teaspoon of milk or pure cream for a darker brown finish if you like).

6. Bake for 15–20 minutes or until the pastry is golden and crispy.

7. Set turnovers aside to cool slightly. Dust with icing sugar and serve with a scoop of vanilla ice cream or a spoonful of dollop cream.

CHAPTER 5

Flavour Foundations

STOCKING THE PANTRY

If you're anything like me and have very limited pantry space, stocking the essentials and removing unnecessary ingredients is a must (my pantry is also my laundry). Having these pantry essentials will provide you with a strong foundation to create a wide range of dishes, especially if you can't be bothered to go to the shops.

Grains and Pasta

○ **Rice:** A versatile base or accompaniment for many dishes. You'll need the right type for the dish, such as long-grain white rice (jasmine or basmati for SE Asian or Indian dishes respectively). Arborio rice for risotto and sushi rice for sushi. Brown rice if you like.

○ **Pasta:** Have a few shapes, such as spaghetti, penne or fusilli. This pantry essential is great for quick meals and to bulk up soups.

○ **Couscous:** It's prepared in just a few minutes and is perfect for salads, sides or as an accompaniment for stews.

○ **Rolled oats:** Have for breakfast, or use in baking and smoothies.

Canned and Jarred Goods

○ **Canned tomatoes:** These are either whole, or crushed/diced. Great for sauces, stews and soups.

○ **Canned beans:** Keep a variety on hand if you have space. I like black beans, chickpeas, red kidney beans and cannellini beans. They are an easy way to add protein to soups, salads, tacos or curries.

○ **Coconut milk and/or cream:** Essential for curries, soups and smoothies.

○ **Canned tuna or salmon:** Fast protein for salads, sandwiches or pasta dishes.

Oils and Vinegars

○ **Extra virgin olive oil:** Perfect for sautéing, for dressings or just drizzling over dishes.

○ **Vegetable or canola oil:** A neutral oil for frying, baking and stir-frying.

○ **Sesame oil:** Great for adding flavour to Asian-inspired dishes such as stir-fries, or in dressings.

○ **Apple cider vinegar:** A tangy addition to dressings or marinades, or use to deglaze pans.

○ **Balsamic vinegar:** Adds sweetness and acidity to dressings, glazes and roasted vegetables.

○ **Rice wine vinegar:** Essential for Asian dishes like sushi rice and dressings.

Baking Staples

○ **Flour:** You'll need plain and self-raising. Use in baking, for thickening sauces or making doughs.

○ **Cornflour:** Great to thicken sauces in an instant, and to make the crispiest fried food.

○ **Sugar:** I use mainly caster and brown sugar. Caster has a fine texture which dissolves easily, and brown sugar adds a slightly caramelised flavour.

○ **Baking powder and bicarbonate of soda (aka bicarb):** These aren't interchangeable, so use the right one for the job. Baking powder is specifically for leavening (raising) baked goods. Bicarb is added to some recipes, usually containing an acid, which creates bubbles and does have a slight leavening effect. It also makes baked goods brown nicely.

○ **Yeast:** Use dry yeast, which comes in 7 g sachets (equivalent of 2 teaspoons). You'll need it for making bread and pizza dough.

○ **Vanilla extract:** This is more concentrated than essence, and gives lovely flavour to baking, sweet dishes and smoothies.

○ **Dutch processed cocoa powder:** Use in baking, smoothies, or adding a deep flavour to sauces (like chilli con carne).

WHAT'S IN MY SPICE RACK?

This is everything I keep stocked in my spice rack in order of how often I use them, plus a few time-saving spice mixes to keep on hand.

Every Day
- ○ Garlic powder
- ○ Onion powder
- ○ Smoked paprika
- ○ Chilli powder
- ○ White pepper

Weekly
- ○ Oregano
- ○ Basil
- ○ Thyme
- ○ Rosemary
- ○ Cayenne pepper
- ○ Ground cumin
- ○ Ground coriander
- ○ Dried chilli flakes
- ○ MSG

Occasionally
- ○ Ground turmeric
- ○ Mustard
- ○ Sesame seeds
- ○ Ground ginger
- ○ Fennel seeds
- ○ Ground cinnamon
- ○ Curry powder

Rarely (but it's good to have)
- ○ Allspice
- ○ Celery salt
- ○ Chinese five spice
- ○ Ground cloves

SPICE MIXES

Don't bother buying spice mixes, which can contain preservatives and other undesirable ingredients. Make your own and keep them (clearly labelled!) in airtight containers in a cool dark place for up to 3 months.

Fajita Seasoning

- 40 g cornflour
- 40 g chilli powder
- 20 g salt
- 25 g smoked paprika
- 20 g caster sugar
- 10 g onion powder
- 10 g garlic powder
- 15 g ground cumin
- 10 g cayenne pepper

Mexican Spice Blend

- 45 g chilli powder
- 18 g ground cumin
- 10 g paprika (smoked or regular)
- 10 g garlic powder
- 5 g onion powder
- 3 g dried oregano
- 3 g salt
- 1.5 g ground black pepper
- 1.5 g dried chilli flakes

Italian Blend

- 40 g dried basil
- 40 g dried thyme
- 25 g dried oregano
- 25 g dried rosemary
- 25 g garlic powder
- 5 g onion powder
- 5 g salt

Cajun Spice

- 40 g cumin
- 40 g ground coriander
- 40 g paprika
- 20 g dried oregano
- 10 g salt
- 10 g ground black pepper
- 10 g cayenne pepper

Garam Masala

- 15 g ground cumin
- 10 g ground coriander
- 5 g ground cardamom
- 8 g ground cinnamon
- 2 g ground cloves
- 2 g ground black pepper
- 2 g ground nutmeg
- 2 g ground turmeric

Italian Blend
Cajun Spice
Garam Masala
Mexican Spice Blend
Fajita Seasoning

STOCKING THE FRIDGE

Failure to prepare is preparing to fail. Having a well-stocked fridge will help you avoid needing to go to the shops for that one ingredient that you're missing for a recipe (a real pain). This is my simple list of fridge essentials, things you should have on hand at all times along with a few recipes for easy enhancers that can elevate any recipe in an instant.

Condiments and Sauces

- ○ **Soy sauce:** This classic sauce adds umami and saltiness; great for stir-fries, marinades and dressings.
- ○ **Worcestershire sauce:** Deep, savoury flavour perfect for meats, stews and dressings.
- ○ **Hot sauce (such as Tabasco and sriracha):** These give a dash of heat to a variety of dishes such as tacos, eggs and soups.
- ○ **Mustard:** Dijon is versatile, but you can also have wholegrain and hot mustard if you like. Great for vinaigrettes, sandwiches, marinades or glazing meats.
- ○ **Balsamic vinegar:** This sweet, tangy vinegar is ideal for salad dressings, roasted veggies and marinades.
- ○ **Mayonnaise:** Use on sandwiches, in dressings, or as a base for dips.

Dairy

- ○ **Butter:** A flavour base for cooking, sautéing or finishing dishes for added richness.
- ○ **Parmesan (or pecorino):** Adds a salty, umami punch to pastas, salads or roasted vegetables. Buy a good quality block and grate it as needed – no pre-grated stuff.
- ○ **Cream:** Thickened cream is versatile, as it is good in cooking and for whipping. Perfect for soups, sauces and creamy dishes.
- ○ **Greek yoghurt:** A thick, tangy, creamy addition to dips and dressings, and as a topping for savoury dishes.
- ○ **Cheese:** You'll need different types for different dishes. Cheddar, mozzarella and feta are great to have on hand. Cheese adds richness and flavour to everything from salads to pasta.

Fresh Produce

- ○ **Lemons:** These are so useful, both for the zest and juice. They add acidity and brightness to any dish – sweet or savoury.
- ○ **Garlic:** Keep as much garlic on hand as humanly possible.
- ○ **Fresh herbs:** My favourites are parsley, coriander, rosemary and thyme, to use in cooking and to sprinkle on for serving. To keep in the fridge, wash the leaves and shake off the excess water. Wrap in paper towel and keep in a plastic bag in the crisper. Even better, keep a few pots of these in the garden, so you can grab a handful anytime. You can also keep bunches on the kitchen bench in glass jars, with water covering the stems. Change the water daily.

Pickled and Fermented Foods

- ○ **Pickled jalapeños or chillies:** These add heat and acidity to sandwiches, tacos or salads.
- ○ **Pickles (dill or bread-and-butter):** Great for sandwiches, burgers or as a side to cut through rich dishes.
- ○ **Kimchi:** Spicy, sour and fermented, it's a flavour powerhouse that can elevate stir-fries, rice bowls or just to eat by itself.
- ○ **Gochujang:** A Korean fermented chilli paste. It is spicy, earthy and slightly sweet.
- ○ **Olives:** These add brininess and umami to pasta dishes, salads and appetisers.
- ○ **Capers:** A little of these goes a long way in adding tangy, briny flavour to salads, pastas or fish dishes.

Pastes and Spices

- ○ **Tomato paste:** This adds concentrated tomato flavour to sauces, soups and stews.
- ○ **Curry paste:** Red, green or yellow for Thai curries, or any of the Indian flavours (such as korma, rogan josh or tandoori). Perfect for a quick curry or to add depth to soups and sauces.
- ○ **Chilli paste or sambal oelek:** For a quick heat addition to stir-fries, sauces and soups.
- ○ **Tahini:** This is ground sesame paste that can be used in dressings, dips (like hummus) or for drizzling on roasted veggies.

Infused Oils

Before we infuse any flavours into oil, there are a few things to be mindful of to keep the oil from going bad. The three enemies of oil are heat, light and moisture, so it's best to store in a cool, dark place. So no, you can't keep it next to your stove (like me) and if possible, it's best to store in a dark glass jar or container. Contact with oxygen also accelerates the degradation process – so use it up! To sterilise bottles or jars, wash well then dry in a low oven.

CHILLI OIL

This chilli oil is a great way to add spice to any dish. Use it as a garnish to add heat and dress the dish with a deep red colour, mixed with some soy sauce for a quick and flavourful dipping sauce for your dumplings or even add it into your curries for an extra kick of spice. This should last up to 3 months, stored in a cool, dark place.

MAKES 2 cups (500 ml)
PREP TIME 10 minutes
COOK TIME 20–30 minutes plus cooling time

½ cup (25 g) dried chilli flakes
2 cups (500 ml) extra virgin olive oil
6 cloves garlic, crushed
5 mm thick slice fresh ginger
3 star anise
1 cinnamon stick
1 golden shallot, thinly sliced

1   Put the chilli flakes into a heatproof bowl and set aside. Pour the oil into a saucepan and add the remaining ingredients (except the chilli flakes). Stir to separate any pieces stuck together.

2   Turn the heat on to medium-low and heat until small bubbles rise, then turn the heat down to low. Heat gently for 20 minutes, until the aromatic vegetables have browned but not burnt and the flavours have infuse into the oil.

3   Strain the oil and discard the solids.

4   Pour the hot oil over the chilli flakes in 3 batches, stirring between each addition to avoid clumping and scorching the chilli flakes. Set aside to cool completely.

5   Use a funnel to pour into a sterilised bottle or glass jar.

HERB OIL

Should I use fresh or dry herbs? Fresh herbs will impart a stronger and more vibrant flavour to your oil but you run the risk of bacteria growth if stored for more than 1–2 weeks. Using dry herbs will result in a more subtle flavour but it can be stored for up to 3 months in a cool dark place or up to 6 months in the fridge. Use this as a garnish for a rich dish like Chicken and Chorizo with Risoni (page 72) to add some freshness.

MAKES 2 cups (500 ml)
PREP TIME 5 minutes
COOK TIME 10–15 minutes

3 sprigs fresh thyme (or 1 tablespoon dried thyme)
3 sprigs fresh rosemary (or 1 tablespoon dried rosemary)
½ bunch fresh oregano, leaves picked (or 1 tablespoon dried oregano)
2 cups (500 ml) extra virgin olive oil

1 If using fresh herbs, wash them then dry thoroughly.

2 Pour the oil into a saucepan and add the herbs. Turn the heat on very low and stir to make sure the oil coats every part of the herb.

3 Gradually heat to 60°C for maximum flavour extraction. Once the oil reaches temperature, remove from the heat immediately and set aside for 30 minutes to cool. Use a funnel to pour into a sterilised bottle or glass jar.

Herb
Oil

BASIL OIL

Infused oils like this are really just a bit of a flex. I definitely won't be adding this to my weekly roster but it's something to pull out of the bag to impress your friends and family. This method can be used with any soft herb (such as basil, parsley or coriander) but my favourite by far is basil. Regardless of which herb you choose, the shelf life of these isn't very long and it should be consumed within a week. Served drizzled over sliced tomatoes, burrata, stir a little into a risotto for an aromatic boost, mix with vinegar or lemon juice for a fresh salad dressing or drizzle over a freshly baked pizza.

MAKES about 1 cup (250 ml)
PREP TIME 10 minutes
COOK TIME 20–30 minutes

2 cups of basil leaves
1 cup (250 ml) neutral oil (canola, vegetable, sunflower)

1. Put the basil and oil into a blender and blitz the life out of it. Blend until the leaves are as finely chopped as your blender can get them.

2. Pour the mixture into a small saucepan and cook on medium-low heat for 20–30 minutes or until the temperature reaches 85°C. This will cook out all of the moisture from the leaves and infuse the colour and flavour into the oil.

3. Pour into a stainless steel mixing bowl and place that bowl into a large one filled with iced water to cool it down.

4. Once cool, strain through cheesecloth or a coffee filter to clarify and you'll be left with perfect basil oil.

5. Use a funnel to pour into a sterilised bottle or glass jar and store for up to a week.

Taking Stock

Making stock at home can be a bit of a mission and I don't expect you to be making it weekly for your regular meals, but learning how to make it is pretty easy and very rewarding. Fresh stock is so much better than store-bought or stock powder because you are making it with fresh ingredients and can control what you put in. Once you understand the process you can swap or add different vegetables and herbs to change the flavour of your stock.

BEEF STOCK

Beef stock is a labour of love. The time and effort that goes into it is definitely returned in the flavour added to any meal you use it in. Apart from the amazing depth of flavour, beef stock is also nutrient dense making it 'healthy'.

MAKES about 2 litres
PREP TIME 20 minutes
COOK TIME 4–6 hours

1.5 kg beef bones (such as marrow bones, oxtail, or a mix of bones with some meat on them)
2 tablespoons olive oil
2 brown onions, quartered (leave skin on for extra colour)
2 carrots, roughly chopped
2 celery stalks, roughly chopped
4 cloves garlic, smashed (no need to peel)
1 tablespoon tomato paste
2 bay leaves
1–2 sprigs fresh thyme (or 1 teaspoon dried thyme)
1 tablespoon black peppercorns

Keep for up to 3 days in the fridge, or divide into usable portions in airtight containers and freeze for up to 6 months.

1. Preheat the oven to 200°C. Place the beef bones into a roasting pan and roast for 30–45 minutes, turning occasionally, until nicely browned. This caramelisation deepens the flavour of the stock.

2. In a large stock pot, heat the olive oil over medium-high heat. Add the onion, carrot, celery and garlic. Sauté for 5–7 minutes, until the vegetables begin to soften and the onions develop a deep brown colour, almost burnt. Stir the tomato paste through the vegetables and cook for 1–2 minutes, allowing it to darken and become aromatic. This will give the stock a deeper colour and richness.

3. Add the roasted beef bones to the pot, then pour in enough cold water to cover the bones and vegetables by about 5 cm. This should be roughly 3–4 litres, depending on the size of your pot.

4. Bring to the boil over high heat. As it heats up, foam and impurities will rise to the surface. Skim these off using a ladle or spoon to ensure a clear stock.

5. Once the stock is boiling and the froth has been removed, reduce the heat to low to maintain a gentle simmer. Add the bay leaves, thyme and peppercorns. Let the stock simmer, uncovered, for 4–6 hours. Check occasionally and add more water if needed to keep the ingredients submerged. The longer you simmer, the more flavour you'll extract.

6. Strain the stock through a fine-mesh strainer or cheesecloth into another pot or large container. Discard the solids.

7. Cool the stock then put in the fridge to chill. Skim off any excess fat (it will set at the top and be easy to remove).

CHICKEN STOCK

Chicken stock feels like a double whammy to me because not only can
you add it to virtually any meal, but if you keep the meat and add some
vegetables you've got the perfect soup for a cold winter's night.

MAKES about 2 litres
PREP TIME 15 minutes
COOK TIME 2 hours

1 whole chicken (about 1.2–1.5 kg) or 1 kg chicken bones
   (carcass, wings, backs, etc.)
2 tablespoons olive oil (if using a whole chicken)
2 brown onions, quartered (no need to peel)
2 carrots, peeled and roughly chopped
2 celery stalks, roughly chopped
4 cloves garlic, smashed (no need to peel)
1–2 bay leaves
1–2 sprigs fresh thyme (or 1 teaspoon dried thyme)
1 teaspoon black peppercorns
1 tablespoon apple cider vinegar (optional, helps
   extract minerals from the bones)

Keep for up to 5 days in the fridge, or divide into
usable portions in airtight containers and freeze
for up to 3 months.

1   If using a whole chicken, heat the olive oil in a large
    stockpot over medium-high heat. Brown the chicken
    on all sides for about 10 minutes. This step adds
    depth and flavour to the stock, but it's optional if
    you're using bones or a carcass. If using just chicken
    bones, omit the oil and add to the pot. Add the onion,
    carrot, celery and garlic.

2   Pour in enough cold water to cover the chicken and
    vegetables by about 5 cm, about 3–4 litres. Add the
    bay leaves, thyme, peppercorns and apple cider
    vinegar (if using).

3   Bring just to the boil over high heat. As it heats up,
    foam and impurities will rise to the surface. Skim
    these off with a ladle or spoon to keep the stock
    clear. Once the stock is boiling, reduce the heat
    to low and let it simmer gently for 1½–2 hours,
    uncovered. During this time, the flavours will develop,
    and the liquid will reduce. Occasionally check the
    stock and skim off any foam that rises to the surface.
    If using a whole chicken, remove the chicken from
    the pot after about 45 minutes, when it's cooked
    through, and let it cool. You can shred the meat for
    another use (like soups, tacos or sandwiches) and
    return the bones to the pot to continue simmering.

4   Strain the stock through a fine mesh strainer or
    cheesecloth into another pot or large container,
    discarding solids.

5   Cool the stock then put in the fridge to chill. Skim off
    any excess fat (it will set at the top and be easy to
    remove).

SEAFOOD STOCK

If you are having a prawn feast, don't throw away the shells and heads.
You can make this prawn stock to use in seafood soups or risottos, level up your
instant ramen or just add some extra 'fishy' depth to any seafood meal.

MAKES about 2 litres
PREP TIME 15 minutes
COOK TIME 1 hour

500 g prawn shells and heads
(from about 12–15 giant king prawns)
1 tablespoon olive oil
1 brown onion, quartered (no need to peel)
2 celery stalks, roughly chopped
1 carrot, peeled and roughly chopped
2 cloves garlic, smashed (no need to peel)
2 tablespoons tomato paste
1 bay leaf
2 sprigs fresh thyme (or 1 teaspoon dried thyme)
1 teaspoon black peppercorns
2 litres cold water

Keep for up to 3 days in the fridge, or divide into
usable portions in airtight containers and freeze
for up to 3 months.

1 In a large stockpot, heat the olive oil over medium
heat. Add the prawn shells and heads and sauté for
about 5-7 minutes, stirring occasionally, until they
turn pink and begin to release their aroma. This step
enhances the flavour of the stock.

2 Add the onion, celery, carrot and garlic to the pot.
Continue to sauté for another 5 minutes, stirring
occasionally.

3 Stir in the tomato paste and cook for 1–2 minutes,
to allow the paste to darken slightly and become
aromatic.

4 Pour in 2 litres of cold water, ensuring the shells and
vegetables are fully submerged. Add the bay leaf,
thyme and peppercorns.

5 Bring just to the boil over high heat. Reduce the heat
to low and simmer gently for 30–45 minutes. The
longer you simmer, the more flavour you'll extract
from the prawn shells. Stir occasionally, and skim off
any foam or impurities that rise to the surface.

6 Strain the stock through a fine mesh sieve or
cheesecloth into another large pot or bowl,
discarding the solids.

7 Let the stock cool slightly then refrigerate.

Garlic
and Herb
Butter

Compound Butters

A compound butter is butter that has been mixed with
different flavourings such as herbs and spices to enhance
its flavour profile. Compound butter can be used to
flavour grilled meats, vegetables, seafood or bread.

COWBOY BUTTER

I'm 99 per cent sure that not a single cowboy has ever made this 'cowboy' butter, but I'm willing to look past that because it's delicious. Use this as a dip for any grilled meat or add a slice and let it melt over the top.

SERVES about 6 (1 tablespoon per serving)
PREP TIME 10 minutes

125 g unsalted butter, softened
2 cloves garlic, crushed
1 tablespoon chopped flat-leaf parsley
1 tablespoon chopped chives
1 teaspoon lemon juice
1 teaspoon dijon mustard
½ teaspoon smoked paprika
¼ teaspoon cayenne pepper (optional)

1 In a medium bowl, combine the butter, garlic, herbs, lemon juice, mustard, smoked paprika and cayenne pepper (if using).

2 Stir everything together until smooth and fully combined. Season with salt and pepper to taste.

3 You can either use the butter as it is, or roll it into a log and chill so you can cut slices. To make a log, place the butter in the centre of a piece of plastic wrap, roll it up tightly and twist the ends. Chill it in the fridge for at least 30 minutes to firm up.

4 Once chilled, slice off pieces of the compound butter to serve.

You can store any leftover compound butter in the fridge for up to a week, or in an airtight container in the freezer for up to 3 months.

GARLIC AND HERB BUTTER

I feel like it goes without saying that garlic and herb butter is going to taste insane. The combination of fresh garlic, creamy butter and fragrant herbs is unmatched. Just wait until you make garlic bread with this bad boy, you'll be doing yourself a favour. Alternatively, drop a slice onto a just-cooked steak to take it to the next level.

SERVES about 12 (1 tablespoon per serving)
PREP TIME 10 minutes plus chilling (optional)

250 g unsalted butter, softened
4 cloves garlic, crushed
2 tablespoons chopped thyme leaves
2 tablespoons chopped rosemary
2 tablespoons chopped basil
1 teaspoon salt (or to taste)
2 teaspoons finely grated lemon zest, for extra
  brightness (optional)

1   Place the butter into a medium mixing bowl. Add the garlic, herbs, salt and lemon zest (if using), season with freshly ground black pepper.

2   Use a fork or a spatula to mix everything together until the butter is smooth and the ingredients are evenly incorporated.

3   Taste the butter and add more salt, pepper or herbs if desired.

4   You can either use the butter as it is, or roll it into a log and chill so you can cut slices. To make a log, place the butter in the centre of a piece of plastic wrap, roll it up tightly and twist the ends. Chill it in the fridge for at least 30 minutes to firm up.

5   Once chilled, slice off pieces of the compound butter to serve.

Chocolate
Fudge
Sauce

Sweet and Savoury Sauces

What is sauce and why is it so important? When I think of sauce, the first thing that comes to mind is tomato or barbecue, but it's so much more than that. A sauce is a liquid or semi-liquid mixture used to enhance the flavour, texture and appearance of a dish. It can be thick or thin, cooked or uncooked and is normally made from ingredients like stock, cream, butter, wine, herbs and spices with optional thickeners (cornflour, roux, xanthan gum). It's important because in most cases it ties the whole dish together by enhancing flavours, improving texture and moisture or balancing components. For example, the sweetness of an apple sauce perfectly complements a salty pork chop.

CHOCOLATE FUDGE SAUCE

I remember an ad that aired when I was a kid for a chocolate ice cream topping that would set hard over the ice cream. This doesn't do that at all, but it makes me feel the same kind of way (hungry). Use this as a topping for your desserts, a dipping for churros or just eat it by the spoonful.

SERVES about 10 (2 tablespoons per serving)
PREP TIME 5 minutes
COOK TIME 10 minutes

395 g can sweetened condensed milk
100 g dark chocolate, roughly chopped
80 g unsalted butter
¼ **cup (60 ml) milk**
1 teaspoon vanilla extract

Store any leftovers in an airtight container in the fridge for up to two weeks.

1   In a medium saucepan, combine the condensed milk, chocolate, butter and milk. Heat over medium-low heat, stirring constantly, until the chocolate is fully melted and the mixture is smooth and well combined.

2   Remove from the heat and stir in the vanilla extract.

3   Let the sauce cool slightly before transferring to an airtight jar or container, leaving the lid off until it has cooled completely. It will last up to 2 weeks in the fridge and up to 3 months in the freezer.

4   Warm gently in the microwave before using. It's perfect to drizzle over ice cream, pancakes or waffles, or even just to dip fruit into.

SALTED CARAMEL SAUCE

Salted caramel sauce has no right tasting as good as it does, especially considering it only has 4 ingredients. It also holds a special place in my heart mainly because every time I make it to use in a video, I end up eating the leftovers with a spoon before I even post the video.

SERVES about 15 (2 tablespoons per serving)
PREP TIME 5 minutes
COOK TIME 15 minutes

300 g caster sugar
135 g unsalted butter, chilled and cubed
¾ cup (180 ml) pure cream
1½ teaspoons sea salt flakes

1 In a medium heavy-based saucepan, heat the caster sugar over medium heat. Stir constantly with a heatproof spatula or wooden spoon until the sugar begins to melt. Once the sugar starts to melt, stop stirring and let it cook undisturbed for about 5 minutes, until it turns a rich amber colour. Sugar can burn very easily so swirl the pan around gently to move the caramel around, so it colours evenly.

2 Carefully add the butter to the pan (it will boil up and release steam so be cautious). Stir gently until the butter is completely melted and incorporated into the caramel, becoming a smooth mixture.

3 Slowly pour in the cream, stirring continuously. Be cautious, as the mixture will bubble up again. Insert a thermometer and continue to cook to your desired consistency:
   - 104°C for a sauce that will remain fluid. Perfect for drizzling on top of desserts
   - 110°C for a more solid caramel that will set in a layer but still soft enough to bite through
   - 118°C for a firm but chewy texture that stays in place. Perfect for caramel apples.

4 Remove the saucepan from the heat and stir in the sea salt. Carefully taste and add more salt if desired for a stronger salted flavour but remember that hot sugar can give you some of the worst burns possible so don't go dipping your fingers in the pot.

5 Allow the salted caramel sauce to cool slightly before serving. It will thicken as it cools.

FRESH BASIL PESTO

Store-bought pesto is alright and there's nothing wrong with using it in recipes – I do it often. My only issue with pesto from the shops is that the basil content is considerably lower than what you would expect, sometimes only 16 per cent basil in 'basil' pesto. If that doesn't convince you to make your own pesto that ACTUALLY tastes like basil, then I don't know what will.

SERVES 4–6 (about 2 tablespoons per serving)
PREP TIME 10 minutes
COOK TIME 5 minutes

20 g pine nuts
80 g fresh basil leaves
20 g finely grated parmesan
2 cloves garlic, crushed
150 ml extra virgin olive oil
½ teaspoon salt (or to taste)
¼ teaspoon freshly ground black pepper (or to taste)

1   In a small dry frying pan, toast the pine nuts over medium heat for about 3 minutes, stirring frequently, until golden and fragrant. Be careful not to burn them, pine nuts will continue to cook once off the heat. Once toasted, remove them from the pan and set aside to cool.

2   In a food processor, combine the basil leaves, pine nuts, parmesan and garlic. Pulse a few times to roughly chop the ingredients.

3   With the food processor running, slowly drizzle in the olive oil until the pesto reaches a smooth, thick consistency. You may need to stop and scrape down the sides a few times to ensure even blending.

4   Add the salt and black pepper, and pulse a few more times to combine. Taste and adjust the seasoning as needed.

5   Transfer the pesto to a jar or airtight container. If you're not using it right away, drizzle a thin layer of olive oil on top to help preserve the vibrant green colour.

CHIMICHURRI

If I had to eat only one meal for the rest of my life it would be steak with chimichurri. The complex flavours in this sauce pair perfectly with any grilled meat. It's tangy, slightly spicy, fresh and herby.

SERVES 6–8 (about 2 tablespoons per serving)
PREP TIME 10 minutes
COOK TIME 0 minutes

1 cup (packed) flat-leaf parsley
½ cup oregano leaves (or 2 tablespoons dried oregano)
4 cloves garlic, peeled
2 tablespoons red wine vinegar
½ cup (120 ml) olive oil
1 teaspoon dried chilli flakes (or to taste)

1   In a food processor, combine the parsley, oregano and garlic. Pulse a few times until the herbs and garlic are finely chopped but not puréed.

2   Add the vinegar, oil and chilli flakes. Pulse again until everything is well combined and the sauce reaches a consistency you like. If you prefer a smoother chimichurri, you can pulse it a few more times.

3   Taste and season with salt and pepper to your liking. You can also adjust the vinegar or oil if you want more tang or richness.

4   Transfer the chimichurri to a small bowl or jar. Let it sit for at least 15–20 minutes to allow the flavours to meld.

Store, covered, in the fridge for up to 3 days. Alternatively, transfer to a freezer-safe container, cover with a layer of olive oil and freeze for up to 3 months.

Chimichurri
Fresh Basil
Pesto

WHOLE EGG MAYONNAISE

I was lucky enough to work with a chef who taught me that mayonnaise isn't made from dairy, which in hindsight is actually really embarrassing. He also taught me how to make it fresh and since then any mayo from the supermarket really isn't as good. You could use olive oil for this but it has a stronger flavour, so I find a neutral oil is best.

MAKES about 1.5 cups
PREP TIME 5 minutes

1 egg, at room temperature
1 cup (250 ml) vegetable oil
1 tablespoon dijon mustard
1 tablespoon white vinegar (or lemon juice)
½ teaspoon salt

1   In a tall, narrow jar (like a mason jar), add the egg, mustard, vinegar (or lemon juice) and salt. Season with white pepper.

2   Pour the oil on top of the egg mixture, making sure the oil completely covers the egg. The key is to have the oil at the top so the immersion blender can start the emulsification process.

3   Insert the immersion blender into the jar, all the way to the bottom. Start blending on low speed, then gradually increase the speed while keeping the blender at the bottom for the first few seconds. You should see the mayonnaise starting to form as you blend.

4   Slowly move the immersion blender up and down in the jar, blending everything together until the mayo is thick and creamy (about 20–30 seconds total).

5   Taste the mayonnaise and adjust the seasoning if necessary. You might want a bit more salt, vinegar or lemon juice.

6   Transfer the mayonnaise to an airtight container.

Store it in the fridge for up to 1 week.

TOUM
(LEBANESE GARLIC SAUCE)

I think toum is a hundred times better than aïoli and
you can't change my mind. I really want to say that
this garlic sauce is perfect with barbecued meats
or on sandwiches, but that's not enough because
toum is just perfect in and of itself. Having this recipe
at your disposal might be dangerous, but only
because of how often you'll want to make it.

SERVES 12–15 (about 2 tablespoons per serving)
PREP TIME 10 minutes

7 large garlic cloves (about 70 g total)
1 teaspoon salt
¼ cup (60 ml) lemon juice
1 cup (250 ml) vegetable oil
¼ cup (60 ml) water

1 Peel the garlic cloves and remove any green sprouts
   from the centre, as they can make the sauce bitter.
   Roughly chop the garlic.

2 In a small food processor, combine the garlic and
   salt. Start pulsing until the garlic is finely minced,
   scraping down the sides of the bowl as needed.

3 With the processor running, slowly pour in the lemon
   juice. Process for 10–15 seconds, until the mixture
   becomes a smooth paste.

4 With the processor running, add the oil very slowly
   in a thin, steady stream. This step is crucial for
   creating the creamy texture. You might need to stop
   occasionally to scrape down the sides.

5 Once the oil has been incorporated and the
   mixture starts to thicken, gradually add the water,
   1 tablespoon at a time, while the processor continues
   running. This helps lighten the texture and emulsify
   the sauce. Continue processing for 3–4 minutes, until
   you have a fluffy, white and airy consistency.

6 Taste and adjust the salt or lemon juice as needed.
   Transfer to an airtight container.

Store in the fridge for up to 2 weeks.

GREMOLATA RELISH

Topping your dish with gremolata does more than add a splash of brightness and freshness, it tells your guests that you have 'class' and you pulled out all the stops. Use this on rich or fatty recipes (like osso buco) because the citrus will cut through the richness and make the meal feel more balanced and less heavy.

SERVES 4–6 (about 1 tablespoon per serving)
PREP TIME 10 minutes

½ cup flat-leaf parsley, finely chopped
1 tablespoon finely grated lemon zest
2 cloves garlic, crushed
1 tablespoon extra virgin olive oil
1 tablespoon red wine vinegar (optional, for a tangy kick)

1. In a small bowl, combine the parsley, lemon zest and garlic.

2. Stir in the olive oil and, if using, the red wine vinegar. The vinegar adds a nice tang, but you can skip it for a more traditional gremolata.

3. Season with salt and freshly ground black pepper to taste.

4. Use immediately or refrigerate for up to a day. It's best served fresh to keep its vibrant flavour.

In the event of leftovers, you can store in an airtight container in the fridge for up to 3 days. The parsley will begin to wilt over time, but it can still be used.

BASIC VINAIGRETTE

You need to learn how to make this basic vinaigrette and stop putting mayonnaise on all of your salads. As far as salad dressings go, this is a really solid one and also a great base to add different flavours to.

MAKES about ¾ cup (180 ml)
PREP TIME 5 minutes

2 tablespoons balsamic vinegar
1 tablespoon fresh lemon juice
1 teaspoon dijon mustard
  (or mustard of your choice)
½ cup extra virgin olive oil

1 In a clean screw-top glass jar (such as a mason jar), combine the vinegar, lemon juice and mustard. Add a pinch of salt and freshly ground black pepper.

2 Pour in the olive oil.

3 Seal the jar tightly and shake vigorously for 15–20 seconds, or until the vinaigrette is fully emulsified and has a creamy consistency.

4 Open the jar and taste the vinaigrette. If you'd like it tangier, add a little more lemon juice (or a small dash of balsamic vinegar). If it needs more salt or pepper, adjust accordingly, then shake again to combine.

5 Drizzle over your favourite salads, roasted veggies, or use as a marinade for meats or seafood.

Store any leftover vinaigrette in the jar in the refrigerator for up to a week. Shake well before each use.

Tomato
Sauce

Barbecue
Sauce

HOMEMADE TOMATO SAUCE

I was a 'tomato sauce on everything' kid. Chicken nuggets, hot dogs, meat pies and
sausage rolls always got a dip in the red. I'm glad I grew out of that; it would have been
difficult to get people to watch my cooking videos if everything was served with a side
of Heinz. If tomatoes are not in season, make with 2 cans of crushed tomatoes.

MAKES 3 cups (710 ml)
PREP TIME 10 minutes
COOK TIME 35–40 minutes

1 tablespoon olive oil
1 brown onion, finely chopped
500 g fresh tomatoes, cored, roughly chopped
½ cup (125 ml) apple cider vinegar
¼ cup (55 g) brown sugar
½ teaspoon salt
¼ teaspoon onion powder
¼ teaspoon garlic powder
¼ teaspoon smoked paprika
¼ teaspoon ground cinnamon
1 tablespoon honey

This can be kept, sealed, in the fridge for up to 3 weeks.
If it lasts that long.

1   Heat the oil in a medium saucepan over medium
    heat. Add the onion and sauté for 5–7 minutes,
    stirring occasionally, until the onion becomes soft
    and translucent. The longer you caramelise the
    onion the sweeter and richer the sauce becomes.
    To maximise the flavour you can slowly cook the
    onion until deeply golden brown, if you have time.

2   Purée the tomatoes in a food processor. Add to the
    pan along with the apple cider vinegar and stir
    to combine. Bring the mixture to a simmer, stirring
    occasionally, scraping the sides to avoid burning.

3   Add the sugar, salt, onion powder, garlic powder,
    smoked paprika and cinnamon. Stir well to combine
    and dissolve the sugar. Reduce the heat to low and
    let the mixture simmer for 20–25 minutes, stirring
    occasionally, until thickened and the flavours get
    to know each other. If the sauce thickens too much,
    you can add a small splash of water to reach your
    desired consistency.

4   Cool slightly, then transfer to a large blender and
    blend until smooth. If you don't have a full-sized
    blender and only have a blender cup make sure the
    sauce has cooled down completely before blending,
    because the heat can create pressure and the
    sauce splash out when you unscrew the lid (be safe).

5   Taste and adjust the seasoning as needed. If you
    like it sweeter, add a bit more sugar or honey. If you
    prefer more tang, add a bit more vinegar. You can
    also add extra spices like a pinch of cayenne pepper
    for heat.

6   Let the tomato sauce cool to room temperature
    before transferring it to a clean jar or bottle.

HOMEMADE BARBECUE SAUCE

The age-old debate about tomato vs barbecue sauce is over because this recipe
will change your perception of sauce yada yada yada. It's barbecue sauce and it's
good. I want you to take this recipe and tweak it to make your own perfect sauce. If
you like it sweeter, make it sweeter, add 1 teaspoon of liquid smoke, go crazy.

MAKES 2 cups (494 ml)
PREP TIME 5 minutes
COOK TIME 20 minutes

1 cup (250 ml) tomato sauce
½ cup (140 g) American mustard
¼ cup (60 ml) apple cider vinegar
2 tablespoons brown sugar
1 tablespoon Worcestershire sauce
1 tablespoon smoked paprika
1 teaspoon garlic powder
1 teaspoon cayenne pepper
1 teaspoon honey
1 teaspoon onion powder

1 Combine all the ingredients in a medium saucepan.
   Stir over medium heat until the sugar has dissolved
   and the ingredients are fully combined. Bring the
   mixture to a simmer, then reduce the heat to low.

2 Let the sauce simmer gently for about 15–20 minutes,
   stirring occasionally. This will allow the flavours to
   combine together and the sauce to thicken. If the
   sauce becomes too thick, you can add a small splash
   of water to thin it out to your desired consistency.

3 Taste the sauce and adjust the seasoning if needed.
   If you like it sweeter, add a bit more honey or brown
   sugar. For more tang, add a little more vinegar. If you
   want more heat, increase the cayenne pepper or
   add a bit of hot sauce.

4 Let the sauce cool to room temperature before using.

Store in an airtight container or jar in the refrigerator for up
to 3 weeks.

"""

SHOPPING TIPS

Ordering stock in a cafe isn't really anything like doing a weekly grocery shop for home but there are a few key practices that we can adopt to help make our weekly or bi-weekly grocery shop a breeze.

HOW TO WRITE A GROCERIES LIST

There is an art to writing the perfect shopping list, so think of these as the 10 commandments of groceries. Follow these rules and you'll be spending less time at the shops and more time doing the things you love, like cooking.

1. Review Your Weekly Meals

Before you write your grocery list, know what you'll be cooking. This helps ensure you buy only what you need and reduces impulse purchases.

> **RULE:** Plan out your meals for the week, including breakfast, lunch, dinner and snacks.

Check if any ingredients can be used in multiple meals (e.g. spinach for a salad and a smoothie).

2. Check What You Already Have

Take stock of your pantry, fridge and freezer. This helps avoid buying items you already have, which saves money and space.

> **RULE:** Look through your pantry, fridge and freezer to see what you have in stock.

Make note of items that are running low or about to expire and need replenishing.

3. Organise by Categories

Create your list based on categories to make shopping faster and more efficient. Group items by where they are located in the store (produce, dairy, pantry, etc.).

> **RULE:** Organise your list into categories:
> - Produce (fruits, vegetables, herbs)
> - Dairy (milk, cheese, yoghurt)
> - Proteins (meat, tofu, beans, eggs)
> - Pantry Staples (grains, canned goods, spices, oils)
> - Snacks and convenience (chips, crackers, drinks)
> - Frozen (frozen vegetables, fruits, meat)

Write the most perishable items first, then work your way through longer-lasting items.

4. Stick to the Essentials

Avoid the temptation of buying extra 'just in case' items, or snacks you don't need. Be disciplined about buying only what's necessary for your meals.

> **RULE:** Only add items you will *actually use* for your planned meals or snacks.

If something is not on your list, resist the urge to grab it unless it's a staple you use often (such as olive oil or salt).

5. Add Non-Food Items

Don't forget household essentials like cleaning supplies, paper goods and toiletries. Add these to the list after food items.

> **RULE:** Add non-food items like toiletries, cleaning supplies and other household necessities to the end of the list.

Have a separate section for non-food items to make sure they don't get missed.

6. Double-Check for Ingredients You've Forgotten

Before you finish the list, double-check your meal plans and the recipes you'll be making. Make sure you have all the ingredients and note any extras, like spices or seasonings.

> **RULE:** Quickly review your planned meals and cross-check ingredients.

If you're trying a new recipe, double-check the recipe to ensure you have all ingredients.

7. Be Flexible

Sometimes stores don't have everything you need, or you might find great deals. Be open to substitutes but have a backup plan.

> **RULE:** Keep a flexible mindset; it's okay to adjust if something is unavailable.

Have a substitute in mind (if your recipe calls for fresh basil and it's not available, use dried basil or another herb).

8. Group Similar Items Together

When writing the list, try to group items within the same category, so you don't have to backtrack in the store.

> **RULE:** Write down similar items together in a logical order (produce, dairy, frozen, etc.).

If you're familiar with the layout of your grocery store, write your list in the order of the aisles.

9. Stick to Your Budget

Keep your budget in mind as you write your list and try to stick to it. If necessary, adjust by substituting more expensive items or cutting unnecessary purchases.

> **RULE:** Keep track of how much you're spending and adjust your list accordingly.

Prioritise essentials and limit extra "treat" items if you're on a budget.

10. Keep Your List Handy

If you think of an item throughout the week, add it to your list right away. Carry the list with you to the store to avoid forgetting anything.

> **RULE:** Always add items to your list as you think of them.

Use a grocery list app on your phone for easy, on-the-go updates, or keep a running list on your fridge.

EXAMPLE OF A WELL-ORGANISED GROCERY LIST:

Produce:
- 6 bananas
- 1 bunch parsley
- 2 carrots
- 1 avocado

Dairy & Eggs:
- 3L milk
- 6 eggs
- 1 packet shredded cheese

Proteins:
- 2 chicken breasts
- 1 can black beans
- 2 scotch fillet steaks

Pantry Staples:
- 1 bag rice
- 1 jar passata
- 1 bottle olive oil
- 1 jar peanut butter

Frozen:
- 1 bag chicken nuggets
- 1 bag frozen mixed berries

Snacks:
- 1 box muesli bars
- 1 bag tortilla chips

Non-Food Items:
- 1 bottle dish soap
- 1 toilet paper pack

HOW TO MEAL PLAN

Writing a meal plan for the week might seem difficult at first but the hardest meal plan is the first one you write. Follow this guide to streamline your weekly meal shopping and get excited for what used to be 'boring and basic' weeknight meals.

1. Be Intentional, Set Your Goals

- **Health Goals:** Are you focusing on weight loss, muscle gain, improving your overall health, or just trying to eat more balanced meals?
- **Budget Goals:** Decide how much you're willing to/or can spend on groceries this week.
- **Time Constraints:** Consider how much time you have for cooking each day. Do you need quick meals or can you invest more time into cooking?

2. Assess Your Pantry and Fridge

- Before planning your meals, check what ingredients you already have at home. This prevents buying duplicates and helps reduce waste.
- Make note of perishable items that need to be used soon, so you can plan meals around them.

3. Pick Your Meals for the Week

- **Breakfast:** Pick 2–3 breakfast options that you can rotate throughout the week. These could be simple (overnight oats, smoothies, scrambled eggs) or more elaborate (pancakes, breakfast burritos).
- **Lunch:** Think about making batches of salads, taco bowls, wraps or soups that you can easily pack for work or eat at home.
- **Dinner:** Choose a few main dishes you want to cook, aiming for a variety of cuisines (Italian, Mexican, Asian) balancing protein, carbs and vegetables. Consider repeating meals on certain days to make your week easier.
- **Snacks:** Choose snacks that are easy to prepare and store (nuts, yoghurt, muesli bars, fruit).
- **Treats:** If you want to include desserts or indulgent snacks, plan those as well. Maybe choose something from chapter 4?

4. Create a Grocery List

- Write down all the ingredients you'll need for your planned meals. Organise the list by categories.
- Don't forget the basics like seasonings, oils and condiments that you might need to restock.

5. Prep in Batches

- Cook in batches: If possible, cook certain ingredients (grains, proteins, veggies) in large quantities to be used in multiple meals throughout the week.
- Prep ingredients: Wash, chop and store fruits and vegetables, portion out snacks, or marinate proteins ahead of time.
- Portion control: Consider portioning out meals or ingredients in individual servings for easier grab-and-go options. This doesn't mean counting calories or weighing your chicken breast, but having meals ready to eat that don't need any further effort.

6. Choose Easy-to-Prepare Recipes

- If you're tight on time during the week, choose recipes that require minimal prep and cooking time, or ones you can make in bulk (like casseroles, stews or stir-fries).
- Have a mix of quick, easy meals and ones that can be batch-cooked or prepped ahead of time for later in the week. If you need inspiration, head to chapter 3.

7. Plan for Leftovers

- Think ahead about which meals can be easily repurposed. For example, roast a chicken for dinner and use leftovers for salads or sandwiches the next day.
- Use leftovers creatively to save time and reduce waste.

8. Make a Cooking Schedule

- Break down when you'll cook each meal: which meals will be prepared in advance (meal prep day), and which will be cooked fresh.
- Plan time for mid-week replenishing (making fresh salads or roasting another batch of vegetables).

9. Stay Flexible

- Life happens. If a day gets busy, have backup options (like frozen meals, takeaway or simple snacks) ready to go.
- Swap meals around if you're craving something different.

10. Review and Adjust Each Week

- At the end of the week, reflect on what worked and what didn't. Did you run out of lunch options? Did you overbuy ingredients? Did you get sick of eating out of Tupperware? Adjust for next week based on what you learned, such as planning more simple meals to cook fresh during the week, to avoid getting sick of the same meals.
- Track your grocery spending to ensure you're staying within budget.

SEASONAL PRODUCE

Plan your meals around seasonal produce! There are a number of reasons why you should keep seasonal produce in mind when thinking about what to cook for dinner (or for the week). Not only do fruits and vegetables taste better when they are in season, but they are also cheaper. 'In season' produce is typically higher in nutrition too, due to being picked at its peak, leading to less nutrient loss during transportation and storage.

Grilled Peach and Burrata Salad with a Honey-Lemon Dressing

Planning your meals around what's in season can also allow you to try new meals and diversify your cooking knowledge. Here's a recipe using Australian seasonal produce around December.

SERVES 2–3
PREP TIME 10 minutes
COOK TIME 3–4 minutes

2 ripe peaches
handful of fresh basil leaves,
    plus extra to serve (optional)
handful of mixed greens (such as
    rocket, spinach, or baby lettuce)
1 Lebanese cucumber, sliced
250 g cherry tomatoes, halved
100 g burrata
DRESSING
1 tablespoon honey
2 tablespoons extra virgin olive oil
1 tablespoon fresh lemon juice

1   Cut the peaches in half and remove the stones. Heat a barbecue grill or char-grill pan over medium-high heat. Place the peach halves on the grill, cut side down, and grill for 3–4 minutes, until grill marks form and the peaches soften slightly. Remove from heat and set aside to cool.

2   To make the dressing, place the ingredients into a clean screw-top glass jar. Seal the jar tightly and shake until evenly combined. Season with salt and freshly ground black pepper.

3   Place the basil and mixed greens into a large salad bowl.

4   Slice the grilled peaches and add them to the salad bowl, along with the cucumber and tomatoes. Tear or chop the burrata into smaller chunks and add to the salad. Drizzle the dressing over the top and toss gently to combine.

5   Serve immediately, topped with extra basil leaves if desired.

CONVERSIONS

As an Australian learning to cook online it's honestly the biggest pain in the a** trying to convert Freedom units (imperial) to their correct state (the metric system). So, I'm going to make it a whole lot easier for you with a cheat sheet. Next time a recipe asks for 2.2 pounds of ground beef you can come back here and find out that it's 1 kg (that sounds 2.204 times easier to me).

Liquid Volume Conversions

Tsp	Tbsp	Ounces	Cups	Quarts	Gallons	Millilitres	Litres
3	1	½	¹⁄₁₆			15	0.015
12	4	2	¼			60	0.06
24	8	4	½			125	0.125
48	16	8	1	¼	¹⁄₁₆	250	0.25
		16	2	½	⅛	500	0.5
		32	4	1	¼	950	0.95
		128	16	4	1	3800	3.8

Dry Weight Conversions

Ounces	Tbsp	Cups	Lbs (pounds)	Grams
1 oz	2 Tbsp	⅛ cup	0.0625	28 g
2 oz	4 Tbsp	¼ cup	0.125	57 g
4 oz	8 Tbsp	½ cup	0.25	115 g
8 oz	16 Tbsp	1 cup	0.5	227 g
12 oz	24 Tbsp	1½ cups	0.75	340 g
16 oz	32 Tbsp	2 cups	1	455 g
32 oz	64 Tbsp	4 cups	2	907 g
			2.204	1000 g (1 kg)

Oven Temperature conversions

Celsius (C)	Fahrenheit (F)
130°C	250°F
165°C	325°F
177°C	350°F
190°C	375°F
200°C	400°F
220°C	425°F

SUBSTITUTIONS TABLE

'When life gives you lemons, make lemonade.' But what if I don't have lemons? Say no more, this table is full of food substitutes. For whatever reason, sometimes we just don't have an ingredient for the recipe we want to make and that's okay, I'm here to help you.

If you don't have this	You can use this
1 teaspoon bicarb soda	4 teaspoon baking powder
1 teaspoon baking powder	¼ teaspoon bicarb soda, ¼ teaspoon cornflour + ½ teaspoon cream of tartar
1 teaspoon lemon juice	½ teaspoon vinegar
1 tablespoon gelatine	2 teaspoons agar agar
1 cup cream cheese	1 cup low fat ricotta cheese
1 cup stock (chicken or beef)	1 tablespoon soy sauce + 1 cup water
1 cup mayonnaise	1 cup sour cream/plain yoghurt/puréed cottage cheese
1 tablespoon cornstarch	2 tablespoons plain flour
1 cup honey	1¼ cup sugar + ½ cup oil/water or 1 cup maple syrup
1 cup brown sugar	1 tablespoon molasses + 1 cup caster sugar
1 cup unsalted butter	1 cup margarine or 1 cup vegetable shortening
30g unsweetened chocolate	1 tablespoon cocoa powder + 1 tablespoon unsalted butter
1 cup buttermilk	1 tablespoon lemon juice + 1 cup milk, 1 cup plain yoghurt
1 teaspoon vanilla extract	1 teaspoon maple syrup, 1 teaspoon almond extract
1 cup red wine	1 cup beef stock
1 cup white wine	1 cup chicken stock
1 tin (395 g) sweetened condensed milk	½ cup caster sugar + ½ cup dark brown sugar
½ cup soy sauce	¼ cup Worcestershire sauce + 1 tablespoon water

GLOSSARY

AL DENTE

An Italian term meaning 'to the tooth' – describes pasta, rice, or vegetables that are cooked until just tender but still slightly firm when bitten.

BUTTERFLY

To cut meat or seafood almost in half, then open it like a book – often done to make it thinner and more even for quick cooking.

CARAMELISED

When sugars in food brown through cooking, creating a sweet, nutty, deep flavour – happens with onions, meat or even desserts.

CARTOUCHE

A round piece of parchment paper placed directly on the surface of food as it cooks – helps trap moisture and control evaporation in slow-cooked dishes.

DEGLAZE

To add liquid (like wine, broth or water) to a hot pan after searing to loosen and dissolve the browned bits stuck to the bottom – these bits add deep flavour to sauces.

EMULSIFY

To combine two ingredients that normally don't mix (like oil and water) into a smooth, uniform mixture – often by whisking or blending. Common in dressings, sauces and toum.

FOLD

A gentle mixing technique used to combine ingredients (like whipped cream or egg whites) without deflating them – done with a spatula in a lifting and turning motion.

FOND

The golden-brown bits stuck to the bottom of a pan after sautéing or searing – full of flavour and often deglazed into sauces.

FRAGRANT

A cue in recipes that signals when ingredients like garlic, spices or herbs have released their aroma – often means it's time for the next step.

ROUX

A cooked mixture of equal parts fat (like butter) and flour, used to thicken sauces, soups or gravies.

RUSTIC

A cooking or presentation style that's hearty, simple, and imperfect – think chunky textures, torn herbs and natural shapes.

SAUTÉ

To cook food quickly in a small amount of oil or butter over medium-high heat, usually to soften vegetables or add flavour through browning.

SEAR

To cook the surface of food (usually meat) over high heat until browned – locks in flavour and creates a tasty crust.

SEASON

To enhance food's flavour by adding salt, pepper, herbs or spices – usually done throughout the cooking process, not just at the end.

SOFT PEAKS

Whipped cream or egg whites that form peaks when the whisk is lifted, but the tips gently curl over – softer and less firm than stiff peaks.

STIFF PEAKS

Whipped cream or egg whites that hold their shape firmly when the whisk is lifted – the peaks stand straight up without drooping.

ACKNOWLEDGEMENTS

Firstly I would like to say an enormous thank you to my managers at Amplify. Emily, this book wouldn't have ever made it past the pitch without all of your hard work. Thank you so much for keeping me on track, providing me with creative direction and genuinely being interested and invested in my success. That being said, this book is just as much yours as it is mine. To everyone else at Amplify, I appreciate the environment you have created more than you know. Alex and Tom, thank you for giving me the opportunity all those years ago to grow to where I am right now. It's pretty crazy to think about how far I've come with you guys from trying to be an edgy comedian to writing my own cookbook.

To Pascal, thank you for sharing your knowledge and experience with me. You've done more than just teach me how to cook: every life lesson I learnt working with you will stay with me for the rest of my life. Thank you for your patience (most of the time) and for supporting my ambitious career choice. I really hope this book reflects everything you taught me – love you, mate.

To Ashwin Khurana, thank you for giving me the opportunity to create something this huge. I would have never thought in a million years that I would be able to write a cookbook, but your support and guidance throughout this whole process made everything so much easier for me. Another huge thank you to Jodie Ramodien! Thank you for working so hard editing this book, picking up and fixing every error I made and making it seem like I know how to put a sentence together. I really appreciate the time both of you gave to me throughout the writing, shooting and editing process of this book!

To William Meppem and Lucy Tweed, I am so grateful to have had such an amazing team for the sprint of a 10 day shoot. You two are so inspiring with the work you have produced. Will, your photography brought the recipes to life in a way I would have never imagined, you're so talented and it was an absolute pleasure to work in your studio, thank you so much! And Lucy, I still can't understand how you style food, it's an enigma. The way you made the recipes look so real was amazing. Thank you for stepping in and helping me cook (and by that I mean I did nothing for 10 days). You two both turned the recipe shoot from one of the scariest things I've ever done into such an exciting and fun time. I really hope I get the opportunity to work with you again in the future. Thank you so much!

To my amazing girlfriend, Abbie, thank you for always supporting me in everything I do. You've always been there to reassure me when I doubt myself and I will never be able to thank you enough.

And finally thank you to YOU. To anyone who has watched my content, liked or commented on a video, thank you! It's you guys who have gotten me to where I am and made this book possible. I said it before and I'll say it again, I never in a million years thought that I would be able to write a cookbook but here it is. Thank you all so much and I hope you love the book as much as I loved making it. Let's cook!

INDEX

Powered by Penguin

Looking for more great reads, exclusive content and book giveaways?

Subscribe to our weekly newsletter.

Scan the QR code or visit penguin.com.au/signup